The New Fashion Rules

Inthefrow

The New Fashion Rules

VICTORIA MAGRATH

HarperCollinsPublishers

HarperCollins*Publishers*
1 London Bridge Street
London SE1 9GF

www.harpercollins.co.uk

First published by HarperCollins*Publishers* 2018

3 5 7 9 10 8 6 4

A catalogue record of this book is available from the British
Library

HB ISBN 978-0-00-830555-0
EB ISBN 978-0-00-830556-7

Printed and bound in Latvia

MIX
Paper from
responsible sources
FSC™ C007454

FSC™ is a non-profit international organisation established to promote the
responsible management of the world's forests. Products carrying the FSC
label are independently certified to assure consumers that they come from
forests that are managed to meet the social, economic and ecological needs
of present and future generations, and other controlled sources.

Find out more about HarperCollins and the environment at
www.harpercollins.co.uk/green

For the fashion students, the enthusiasts, the creatives, the bosses, the marketers, the online shoppers, the clothing admirers, the fashion show attendees, the writers and the devoted fans of the fashion world.

Your passion is my passion. This one's for you.

Contents

Introduction

Who decides what we wear, how we dress and the way we define ourselves through clothing? Is it us? Do we decide our own take on style and self-branding? Or is it our audience, the passer-by in the street, the person in front of us in the coffee queue or our latest follower on Instagram? The rules of the fashion game have changed, and we are all having to learn the new tips, tricks and rules to play it successfully.

We live in a world where the majority dress to fit in with societal norms, and our clothing can offer an insight into our status, character, interests and our sense of what's appropriate and what's not. As humans, we have always loved to fit into a group to feel a sense of belonging, but the recent evolution of the Internet has had the most dramatic effect on the way we dress today. It has transformed the way fashion is worn,

consumed, sold and produced. The majority of us no longer buy clothing for our own personal enjoyment alone, but for the admiration of those who observe or follow us.

Online fashion retailing has fascinated me since it was kicked up a notch in the early 2000s. I studied for my fashion retail degree at the University of Manchester in 2007 and although online shopping was rising in popularity, lots of people were still dubious that it would ever stick. I was sitting in a branding lecture while my lecturer scoffed at the idea that people would ever risk buying such tactile items on their computer. She believed that buying clothing online would never take off, but I was already seeing a trend: brands were increasingly developing online stores and I knew it was only a matter of time before more people tried it out for themselves.

Before I had finished my degree, mobile-retailing was already a realistic proposition and within a small space of time, the thought of shopping on my mobile became somewhat normal. Retailers not only had an online store to sell their products globally, but they could now promote and sell them from every mobile phone in the world. The question at that point was how exactly could a brand entice people to buy from their mobile app, and what could they do to enhance their customers' enjoyment and experience? I was intrigued, so I started a three-year PhD to answer that very question.

My thesis investigated the purchasing decisions, behaviours and emotions of the fashion consumer shopping on mobile apps. After three fun and interesting years, I graduated, added 'Dr' to my title and found out that mobile retailing would actually be far more lucrative and essential for retailers than we had initially expected (among a lot of other things, of course, but we don't have all day). But my findings were borne

out over the following eight years, backed up by stats published in 2017, stating that 58 per cent of ASOS's sales came from mobile purchases, and 70 per cent of their web traffic came via mobile. I'm guessing their mobile site was pretty great ... they must have read my PhD. *I'm joking.*

But let's get back to today, when online retailing is global and no longer solely dependent on the elite who have money to spend. Fashion and style inspiration are no longer being dictated by top models and society's richest from their ivory towers — the latest trends are promoted by ordinary people from their bedrooms. New York blogger and photographer Scott Schuman was one of the first on the scene, documenting the outfits of ordinary people on the streets. His website, The Sartorialist, was the birth of what would soon become a widespread appetite for street-style imagery, and it acted as a catalyst for a new wave of street-style photographers, hungry for well-dressed folk. Now, fashion week shows are swarming with photographers falling over each other to get a snap of the best-dressed attendee — something that not everyone is happy about, but we'll get to that later in the book. The Internet has democratised fashion, so that it's starting to be led by the more relatable girl- or boy-next-door. They take selfies, write blogs and vlog to camera – and while the relationship between fashion and the world's wealthiest people still exists, a broader range of social influencers are flooding the fashion scene.

After my PhD, I took up a lecturing position at the University of Manchester. But, armed with fresh information about a vastly growing industry, I wanted to write it all down, so I started a fashion, beauty and travel blog. Inthefrow – an abbreviation of in the front row – was the name of my bubble, where I offered my readers a portal to the latest clothing I loved, beauty products worth our money and trends to hit the catwalk. I wanted to create 'the digital front row' for a new generation of fashion-hungry readers. At that stage in my career I had no idea that one day my blog would enable me to sit physically on the front row, at shows like Dior, Victoria Beckham, Burberry and Julien Macdonald.

Blogging is one of the biggest additions to fashion media since monthly magazines. While the first female fashion magazine, *The Ladies' Mercury*, appeared in London in 1693, fashion blogging as we know it only erupted in 2006, and has led to the creation of an entirely new career. The blog as a medium has turned a small number of ordinary writers into powerful and influential voices. In fashion, a select few have a reach of over 10 million followers – much larger than any print or fashion magazine – alongside running their own clothing labels, writing their own books and starring in advertising campaigns for some of the largest brands in the world. Bloggers have become brand ambassadors. They strut the catwalks of the most prestigious

designers and adorn the covers of the most established magazines. Again, more of that later in the book.

I'm extremely proud to say, after six years in this business, that I've had a number of these opportunities and have collaborated with some of my favourite brands, both on- and offline. But I am still growing, learning and developing every day, because the evolution of the Internet, and how it shapes the fashion industry, never stops. We all have to continue to adapt to fit in with the new norms, the trend setters, the innovators and the latest innovations.

We've all seen enormous shifts in the way brands and retailers are running their businesses. Fashion is no longer solely consumed on the high street. I remember purposefully going clothes shopping on Wigan high street as a teenager, because unless you ordered from the Next catalogue, there was no other access to a new outfit for a Friday night. Back then you were confined to a handful of clothing stores in your local town or retail park, unless you ventured further afield to your nearest city for a broader range of brands and retailers. In today's digitally-minded world, a customer can buy their clothing from a multitude of online touchpoints, at any time of the day, and have them delivered to their home or place of work within 24 hours. In the centre of London, clothing can now be bought and

delivered to your door in as little as 90 minutes! This ubiquitous freedom has fundamentally transformed how clothes are advertised, sold and purchased, by everyone around the globe.

So, how do you keep up? For consumers, followers, brands and the ordinary person in the street, there are new rules to follow if you want to stay ahead of the fashion game. So much has happened in recent years, from #TimesUp to virtual-reality models, the cry for inclusivity within the industry and the birth of social media influencing our daily wardrobe. The old way isn't working any more; it's been taken over entirely by a brand-new fashion industry, armed with the latest tools, technology and media. And so, we need a new set of rules to follow – for shopping, for styling, for working in the industry and for our own awareness of what's happening behind the scenes.

I'm going to share with you the pivotal moments that I believe have transformed the fashion industry into something entirely new and what exactly this means for you and me. How does it affect our styling choices, how we consume clothing, where we find our inspiration and how we portray ourselves online? There is so much for all of us to learn, and so I'm sharing personal tips, advice, thoughts and ideas that I've never shared anywhere before. If you want to start your own blog or YouTube channel, if you want to up your Instagram game, find the best places for fashion inspo, learn how best to shop luxury or for sale bargains, or if you just want to swot up on all the coolest fashion info from the last 20 years, you're in the right place. There are 40 key moments to discuss and just as many tips and tricks for you to learn and take away to keep you on top of your game.

Carry on reading, learn the new rules and find out what part you have to play in this crazy digital world of fashion.

Be accessible and easy to find

Everyone is gunning for your attention: the blogger you follow on Instagram, the retailer on the high street, the brand email you just found in your inbox, your mate who just WhatsApped you. (Don't get me started on group chats.) In this world, it's about being seen, liked and validated by your followers, it's about standing out and raising your voice above the noise and it's about being found in a place that is unbelievably saturated. For consumers and followers, everything has become so similar and repetitive, meaning that differentiation and individuality goes a long way. Brands and designers are having to change their strategies: going mobile, opening physical stores and building Instagram shops for their social-media audience. It means that consumers can mix it up, create new ideas and try something new. Nothing is off-limits any more; shop the globe, buy an outfit on your mobile, mix and match luxury and high-street brands and show people how you wear it. The world is a very big place and you have the chance to take advantage of every corner of it. So why miss out on the opportunity?

Get ready to
shop the globe

The high street just got huge. Imagine that you have every clothing store in the world at your fingertips, and their goods are just a few days of delivery time away from being on your doorstep. If you lined up every single online clothing store (those worth your money, that is) along a street in your hometown, no doubt that line would be hundreds and hundreds of miles long. But that's technically what we have now. An entire shopping district, ready to be shopped by anyone on a phone or a computer.

It all started in 1994. Retail went global when an American entrepreneur sold a CD to a friend over an encrypted service. It was the first secure transaction ever to happen online and it opened the floodgates for an online explosion.

I can recall the jealousy I felt when school friends of mine headed to Orlando, Florida, every summer with their parents for yet another year at Disney. But it wasn't Florida I was jealous of; it was the clothing they brought home from those trips. Piles and piles of Abercrombie & Fitch. It was affordable, cool, preppy and the UK market just didn't make clothes like that then. (This was before Topshop had risen to the top of its game.) These friends of mine were strutting around in American-based apparel while I was stuck in Tammy Girl and Kappa tracksuits. (First-world problems, I know, but when you're nine years old, these things seem to matter.)

I also remember the first time I personally bought anything online. It was an Alanis Morissette T-shirt from the US. I bought it on her merch site, paid the extortionate amount and received the crappiest-quality T-shirt, but still, I had ventured into a global marketplace for the first time. If I couldn't make it to Florida myself, I would bring the goods to me. So thanks again, Dad, for 'lending' me that £50 back in 2000. You probably kick-started my shopping habits. I also vividly remember the time when my brother accidentally ordered 10 of the same basketball jersey from America. It was when the dial-up connection was so poor that hitting 'purchase' more than once could lead to you owning that item multiple times. My dad was in uproar at first, until a simple email prevented his credit card being charged $1,000.

Shopping the web got easier and easier as the years went on. Online stores became compatible with mobiles, easier to use on your desktop, safer and more secure for transactions. All this, along with discounts and promo codes, incentivised people to try buying online. The more people tried it, the more they realised there were fewer risks to entering their personal information than they'd thought, and of course it lead to some new shopping habits for many. That is definitely what happened to me. Every time I bought online successfully, I became more relaxed about buying, felt a sense of security and was more willing to come back and shop again, because the process was so straightforward. And I wasn't alone in working out this

entirely new selling platform. In 2017, 24 per cent of purchases globally (for everything apart from food) were made online. That's a quarter of everything bought, purchased from an online website and delivered to somewhere in the world.

I'm not surprised the population wants to invest in brands from around the globe and dress in apparel from their favourite stores from another continent. Worldwide deliveries, next-day shipments and ubiquitous shopping have opened up a global market for consumers and brands to take advantage of. And I, for one, am all for it.

My Dream Shopping Street

I started thinking about the analogy I mentioned earlier, about this never-ending shopping street with every single brand imaginable lined up along it. What a dream! But, of course, I'm not a fan of every single brand, so I decided to visualise what my ideal shopping street would actually look like. If I had a mile of road available and I could build any stores I wanted on it, this is what my shopping street would consist of. Coming up with this was one of the most fun things I've ever had to think up, so feel free to do the same!

It would start with Dior. For the special bag, shoes or couture item you or I might love to own, Dior would definitely be my brand of choice.

Next, there would be a few premium high-street favourites: Joseph, Reiss, All Saints, Whistles, J. Crew, Three Floor, Rixo, Me & Em, Ted Baker and Tommy Hilfiger. These are my go-tos for most of my fashion items.

Be accessible and easy to find

25

There would, of course, be a Selfridges store next to a LuisaViaRoma, Matches and Net-A-Porter pop-ups – I don't want to go changing any brand's retail strategy here. These are my favourite luxury online and offline department stores and I can't get enough of the items they stock.

Next to these, a number of my favourite luxury brands for shoes: Stuart Weitzman, Gianvito Rossi, Valentino, Nicholas Kirkwood, Manolo Blahnik, Vetements, Saint Laurent, Malone Souliers, Sophia Webster and Aquazzura.

Then some of my favourites for accessories: a Strathberry store because they deserve to show off their gorgeous bags in more locations. Dolce & Gabbana, Bulgari, Chanel, Céline, Prada, Chloé, Balenciaga, Louis Vuitton and a Mulberry store, because I tend to visit every one of these stores whenever I'm walking by.

Then we would have Max Mara for coats to die for. Self-Portrait for dresses that make me feel wonderful. Burberry for beautiful outerwear and knits. Balmain for statement items that give you the wow factor. Coach for T-shirts, knitwear and beautiful outerwear. Saint Laurent for awesome branded tees. Gucci for clothing with colour and recognisable pattern. Zimmermann and Jonathan Simkhai for the prettiest pieces and Temperley for the most feminine clothing.

There would be a Revolve store for amazing holiday clothes with an LA vibe, as well as a Levi's, Paige, Hudson and GRLFRND Denim for the best jeans ever. Plus a Ray Ban for my sunglasses. If ASOS ever decided to create a store with all of their bestsellers, I'd definitely shop in it. A lot.

An Adidas and a Nike for fitness footwear as well as a Gym Shark pop-up, a Sweaty Betty and a Varley for activewear. I'd get my bikinis and swimwear from Melissa Odabash, Seafolly, PilyQ, Zimmermann, Bond-eye and Mara Hoffman, because they are all totally exquisite and uber-flattering.

I'd also add some of my favourite homeware and lifestyle stores: Urban Outfitters, Zara Home, Made, Oliver Bonas, Anthropologie and & Other Stories.

And because no shopping can be done without refreshment, I'd add Veggie Pret, Pizza East, Farmacy (my favourite Vegan restaurant in Notting Hill), the Burberry Thomas's cafe, Joe & the Juice, Roka for amazing Japanese food and Australasia (my favourite Manchester restaurant), which again cooks up incredible Japanese cuisine.

Throw in the Plaza Athénée hotel and I would never leave this place.

Be accessible and easy to find

ASOS changes the online shopping game

Kate Moss is photographed exiting a hotel in a beautiful black leather jacket in the year 2000. She looks amazing, but the jacket she's wearing is the star of the show. Where can you buy it, and more importantly, where you can buy an affordable alternative that looks just as great? And that cute top that Jennifer Aniston is wearing in the latest episode of *Friends*, season seven. I want it, but I have no idea where to find it and neither do the other 10,000 women who saw the show and also fell in love with it. So sparks the ingenious idea, by Nick Robertson, to create a portal for items As-Seen-On-Screen, and ASOS is launched for every fashion-conscious person in the land. Here you could find and buy fashion alternatives to dress like your favourite star. A commercial idea for a celebrity-adoring population. It was one of the savviest ideas in the history of fashion.

Kate Moss

No other retailer had capitalised on the celebrity-outfit-dupes concept and culture in such an easy and affordable way. And by doing so, ASOS built up a loyal audience who would stick with them when they adapted their strategy to a dynamic fashion retail space.

That was in the year 2000. Sixteen years later, after a number of changes to their strategy, ASOS made £1,403.7 million in retail sales. In 2017, they were the biggest online-only (pure-play) retailer by sales in the world. ASOS were pioneers in an open marketplace, driving new ideas and pushing the boundaries when it came to customer service and shopping experiences. They were forward thinking with their delivery and returns processes (they're the only fashion retailer to offer a year's unlimited next-day delivery for £9.95 regardless of how much you spend), inspirational with their editorial, blog and social content and ingenious with their product-display techniques. I remember when I first stumbled onto ASOS back at university and ten years later, I'm still just as obsessed. I used to have asos.com as my browser's homepage, just so that I could check the 'new in' section every single day before

Be accessible and easy to find

Nick Robertson

I even went to Google. The concierge in my building knew me personally because I would check for new parcels every day, and my flatmates almost had to hold an intervention. Okay, I'm exaggerating a little, but I was definitely mocked repeatedly for how many times a week I would place an order.

Free deliveries and returns, catwalks for every product, style advice, sizing help and one of the biggest catalogues of products on the Internet. There are 4,000 new styles per week! But unlike many online retailers who stock alternative brands, ASOS stocks 44 per cent of its own product too, with 66 per cent of styles being unique to the company. They sell 850 brands and have warehouses in the UK, US and Europe, meaning they can ship to you wherever you are in the world — and that's within a matter of days.

Not charging for returns or delivery was fundamental to the increase in customer acceptance. More people started to use and trust ASOS and this led to more trust in online shopping, encouraging more shoppers to become online purchasers. So the online selling space has a lot to thank ASOS for. It has thrived in its wake and the fashion retail space has never been the same since its launch. Thus, ASOS is definitely one of the biggest retail game-changers of the 21st century.

Be accessible and easy to find

Reasons I love to shop online

1. Free returns – buy both sizes just in case and send back the one that doesn't fit.

2. You never need to leave your house – pyjamas and a coffee in bed, scrolling through a website, is far more relaxing for me than pushing my way through Oxford Street on a Saturday afternoon.

3. Everything is under one roof – if you physically shopped through the rails of every store you can find on ASOS, Net-A-Porter or even Selfridges online, it would take you hours to walk from door to door and shop to shop. Don't get me wrong, I do love to physically shop too, when I'm in the mood, but I'm a converted online shopper through and through.

4. Style advice and ideas – that shirt that you love in the store, it doesn't come with any style advice unless you saw it on a mannequin. Online, the retailer's stylist and merchandisers will have styled it up for you, and hopefully provided links to every other product you can see the model wearing.

Net-A-Porter rides the dotcom boom

Natalie Massenet hit the launch button on her revolutionary new idea. What if the population would like to buy luxury fashion online, from a curated selection of the best premium items in the market? Everyone in the industry had advised her against it. After all, it was only six years since the first item ever was sold online, and for Natalie, everything was riding on this idea being a success. What if no one wanted to spend thousands of pounds on handbags they had never seen in person? And what if the consumer wanted to go into the store to spend their hard-earned salary, rather than trusting an online website? Those questions among hundreds more could have halted Natalie in her tracks and stopped her from publishing the magazine-style shopping website for designer fashion, Net-A-Porter. She could have lost everything from

Natalie Massenet

investing in an idea that may have immediately flopped. But who knew that this venture would lead to 9.5 million orders made in 2017? Without a physical store to show off the products, or a changing room for customers to try them on, selling luxury fashion to an online consumer was risky business. But her gut instinct paid off, and Net-A-Porter is now one of the top 50 online-only retailers in the world. Luxury fashion was online and here to stay.

Net-A-Porter started a trend. It showed the luxury world what could be done and how it could be a success. In its wake, the majority of luxury brands around the world began developing their own online stores. And it wasn't just brands that followed — many companies were also looking to follow in Natalie's footsteps. Mytheresa went online in 2006, Matches Fashion and Farfetch in 2007, Selfridges developed their e-commerce site in 2010 and Monnier Frères in 2011.

Luckily for other entrepreneurs with big ideas, there have been a number of success stories similar to Net-A-Porter. Pure-play retailers have a great advantage in terms of reduced costs on logistics and physical-store overheads, but they also benefit from their exclusivity. Miss it once and it's gone forever. Thus, there are now a multitude of hugely successful, online-only retailers.

Be accessible and easy to find

My favourite online success stories

Black Milk Clothing

Black Milk Clothing launched in 2009 selling colourful, unique leggings to the Australian consumer, swiftly becoming global and building a cult-like following. What started in the founders' kitchen turned into a multi-million-dollar brand with millions of followers and a tribe of loyal customers. And they did it all with zero advertising budget. Word of mouth was all they needed; that, and a global distribution network, a product that was unique in the market and a cool social-media strategy.

Boohoo and Missguided

Boohoo and Missguided are further success stories from the North of England, both developing into huge online retailers with 2.5 million-plus Instagram followers and a foot firmly placed in the high-street retail market. It's not surprising that in 2016 Missguided made £206 million in profits, while Boohoo made £294 million. And luckily for Boohoo, with such staggering profits they were also able to acquire the huge, yet recently bankrupt, American fashion brand Nasty Gal for £20 million.

Revolve Clothing

Revolve Clothing launched in 2003 in the hope of inspiring women with their youthful, Coachella-vibe clothing. Something fresh in a stale market. The brand exploded over the following years, creating an image that isn't in any way replicable. They had a unique vision, took early advantage of the growing influence of bloggers and instagrammers (content-creators) and invested time in girls who would become unofficial ambassadors of the brand. Being part of the Revolve 'family' is cool and idolised, as their strategy involves lavish trips to the Hamptons, Mexico and the Turks and Caicos islands, and, of course, holding their own festival at Coachella. I can vouch for the trips being just as incredible as they look on social media. They set their goals and didn't let up.

Triangl bikinis

Triangl bikinis started in 2012 and now turns over $45 million annually. It succeeded in a relatively unexplored marketplace with beautiful and affordable swimwear that broke the mould. And luckily, it garnered the attention of the likes of Miley Cyrus and Kendall Jenner, leading to a push in sales and a widespread frenzy to buy into the cool Australian brand. It now has over 2.8 million Instagram followers and is one of the most distinguishable swimwear brands in the world.

Luxury for the masses

Whether or not you like to buy your new designer handbag from a boutique, you technically no longer have to. Chanel is one of the only stores to hold out entirely when it comes to selling anything online, and the company apparently doesn't have any plans to change that any time soon. But every other brand, from Aquazzura to Zuhair Murad, stocks most, if not all, of their latest collections somewhere online. The iconic French luxury house of Hermès was surprisingly ahead of the market in April 2001 when they became one of the first luxury brands to launch their own e-commerce site. While back then it was perfumes and small leather goods that you could grab online, after a website refresh and a new strategy in 2017, the heritage brand now stocks almost everything that you can buy in their boutiques – apart from the famous Birkin and Kelly bags, which they will happily help you fall in love with instore.

Be accessible and easy to find

I understand why some may prefer to purchase their latest luxuries online. Shopping in designer stores can often be an intimidating experience. Even when I know I have money to spend, there are times when the eyes of the security guard(s), shop assistants and store manager just feel like they're burning through your not-brushed-this-morning hair. When I was at university, my friends and I would feel out of place going into the Manchester Selfridges store, because we were students and didn't have Gucci hanging off our arms.

It's a big factor for a lot of people. Have you ever felt put off buying an item of clothing or an accessory from a store, because you were on your own and didn't want to venture inside for fear of feeling uncomfortable? I'm sure there would be a show of hands. So many times, my other half, Alex, and I have wandered around luxury houses that I was intending to buy from, and a security guard has followed us because Alex – covered in tattoos, no hair and often in a band T-shirt – doesn't look like a typical designer-brand wearer. Stereotyping at its best.

While Hermès was an early online adopter, the majority of luxury houses only started to move online in around 2012, ultimately making luxury fashion easier to access. A reason, I think, why so many were staying offline as long as they could. Accessibility often equals affordability, and that's not what these stores were selling. Luxury items are supposed to come with an experience, an expectation and a high-quality display. How could the audience obtain those things via an image on a website? But the audience wanted it, and the retailers knew they needed to keep up with the consumer's demand to shop anywhere and at any time.

The service from the majority of these sites is impeccable. I've bought online from Gucci, Dior, Max Mara, Stuart Weitzman and Self-Portrait and my purchases have all been perfectly wrapped and delivered for that perfect luxury, at-home experience. No shopping assistants or awkward glances included.

I adore shopping in luxury boutiques — Dior on Bond Street in London is my favourite store in the world. The interiors, the staff and the layout are just wonderful. But luxury buying has increased dramatically in the past six years or so due to the availability and ease with which you can purchase a pair of £600 shoes and have them delivered to your doorstep. And we will undoubtedly reach a point where everything, even that Hermès Birkin, can be customised, personalised and ordered from your couch at home.

Luxury shopping FAQs

As a blogger with a lust for luxury fashion and beauty, I
often get asked about tips for buying and wearing designer
accessories and clothing. So this is what I often reply to the
top three FAQs:

How should I mix luxury and high street?

Buying an entire wardrobe of designer is not at all necessary.
Great, if you have the disposable income, but not possible
for probably 95 per cent of the world. Plus, you'll be forever

worrying about how best to wash everything you wear. Who has time for that when you just want to throw a white wash in the machine? My favourite way to wear designer clothing is to buy items that you know you will use extensively, that won't need washing every time you wear them and can really enhance your look. For me, this includes bags, shoes and outerwear. The perfect dress I'd add in here too. So blend in your high street pieces: an amazing pair of trousers from ASOS, Topshop or All Saints, throw on a beautiful blouse from Reiss or Whistles and then layer over your new luxury jacket, add that designer bag to your arm and slip into those new designer heels. It's my favourite way to enhance my whole look.

What is it worth spending your money on if you can only afford one luxury item?

If you're looking to buy your first designer item, opt for a bag. It's something you can wear every day, and if you choose the right colour, it will go with everything you own. I would usually suggest a robust, textured leather, black luxury handbag for the first item you invest in, as you can't go wrong. It won't pick up dirt easily, it won't scratch significantly, it will match all of your outfits and you can wear it in any season. Either that or a navy or tan, depending on the colour tones you often wear.

Be accessible and easy to find

If you're not a bag person, go for a pair of shoes. A pair that is appropriate for a lot of weather conditions and won't ruin in the rain if you're caught out without an umbrella. So stay away from suede and choose something in a slightly darker colour if you're spending a lot of money. But if neither shoes nor bags are your thing then I'd suggest a coat. That coat you'll always wear and get so much use out of. I have a navy Gucci wool coat that I couldn't be without and it's seen me through a number of seasons. I also own a few Balmain blazers, including a beautiful white tweed, which add a confident vibe to any outfit and go with pretty much anything in my wardrobe. And then I have a Burberry trench coat that works well in any weather. They're bigger investments, but you'll keep them in your collection forever, and probably hand them down later.

What's your favourite luxury item you've ever bought?

This is a difficult question to answer, as I have only regretted one or two items I've ever bought. I have a Max Mara camel coat that has become a wardrobe staple. When I was younger, I would always look up to the women I saw strutting around in the most sophisticated camel coats, belted at the waist with the collar popped, and I dreamed of a day when I would own one. When that day came and I walked away with the coat of my dreams, I'd never loved an item of clothing more in my life. In my opinion, everyone, male or female, should have a camel coat in their collection.

—

Global connections for the smallest brands

I have found so many incredible, independent brands on my various shopping binges. I often scan the new-in sections of my favourite online department stores to see what's on their rails, and by doing so, I've spotted items I adore from brands I've never heard of. Net-A-Porter, LuisaViaRoma, Selfridges, Matches or Mytheresa; I'll hold up my hands and say that I scour these sites weekly to search for items to fall in love with. I've found beautiful jewellery brands, cool sportswear collections, stunning accessories retailers and even the most established of brands that had somehow previously bypassed my radar. And I don't think I'm alone here. Without these huge online stockists, a lot of brands wouldn't be given the recognition they deserve. It's hard to be acknowledged when the market is saturated with messages and you're not able to shout loud enough. While these sites may take a sizeable cut from the product sales and awareness that they enable, that percentage is probably worth it for brands that otherwise would have to rely on their physical or online store for word of mouth.

We're living in a world of possibilities and opportunities. Anyone can open their own store if they have something worthwhile to sell. Etsy revolutionised the marketplace for individual retailers in June 2005 by providing online storefronts for creative people selling handmade items. I remember the day when my step-dad decided he wanted to pursue a career in woodwork, and suddenly the house was filled with his creations; a beautiful coffee table, a kitchen worktop, shelving units, jewellery boxes, you name it. So I mentioned that he should start an Etsy store. A few years later and he's managed to create and run a successful small business, all from our back-garden work shed.

It's no longer just the largest of companies that are able to thrive. Social media has been a starting point for a number of upcoming brands to grow their business. Just look at Fashionnova and their rise to viral fame after countless social stars were paid to promote their clothing. They now have 12 million Instagram followers and a huge customer base. Whatever the strategy, as long as your product is good and your customers can find you, you've got the world at your feet.

Be accessible and easy to find

Brands I fell in love with online

RIXO

RIXO was founded in 2015 by two London College of Fashion alumni with a love of vintage fashion. Their designs are so recognisable and desired all over the world, and again stocked at Net-A-Porter, which is where I stumbled upon their dresses. The prints and luxurious silks are always impeccable and it's clear they are destined for amazing heights.

Saskia Diez

Saskia Diez is a German jewellery designer who opened her own online store in 2009, but who I personally found on Net-A-Porter in 2017. It is seldom that I buy items from brands that I don't know much about, but I immediately fell in love with the delicacy of her creations and had added a pair of droplet earrings to my basket and checked out within five minutes. I've been hooked on her designs ever since.

Strathberry

Strathberry is a Scottish brand that is taking on the global accessories market. I personally met the owner in 2014 at a press day for new brands and their designs blew me away. But without this chance meeting, the Internet would have been my first introduction, as they were initially based purely online. They are now sold at Selfridges, Saks and Monnier Frères, inevitably opening them up to much wider audiences around the world. I followed their journey after our first meeting, as they followed mine, and we continued to chat and collaborate over the years since. With Meghan Markle becoming an avid fan of their bags, it catapulted the brand even further into the headlines and their bags sold out overnight. At the start of 2018, I launched my own collaboration line of bags and accessories with them, which again sold out overnight, much to my extreme elation. They're bound to grow and grow, and I can't wait to see all of their successes.

Inspiring a love of fashion

Five years ago, my other half didn't own one luxury branded item of clothing. My accessories wardrobe is filled with a number of my favourite brands that I've collected over the years, from Dior to Chanel and Valentino, but my other half just wasn't bothered. He wore his beaten-up Levi's, Vans trainers and assortment of band T-shirts, and that was as far as his brand affiliations went. Which of course is absolutely fine; he rocked his style and it suited him. No one needs to own designer clothes if they're not interested. But over the last couple of years I've noticed him becoming more interested in certain brands and trying new fashion styles. We all adapt our styles as we mature, but if you ask me, or him for that matter, it's all down to the brands and clothing he's seeing on his (or my) Instagram feed. He's exposed to so many more styling ideas:

those cool new trainers that just launched, that awesome logo-heavy hoodie, that new backpack. Fashion inspiration is everywhere – we cannot escape it.

Lookbook.nu was one of the first accounts I signed up to when I started blogging. It launched in April 2008 as a place to share a photo of your outfit, with a description of the items you're wearing, and then other users can like it and comment. This platform is all about the love – no negativity or thumbs down are allowed, because what purpose does that serve? Lookbook was huge in its heyday, inspiring outfit ideas and serving as an image-based blog of sorts. That's before hundreds of thousands of people started their own blogs to post their outfit shots on instead.

Two years later, Pinterest became another haven for those looking for visual advice on what to wear that day. I have scrolled the Pinterest feeds for OOTD (outfit of the day) inspo many a time when I've been at a loss for ideas. Pinterest's filtering system is particularly useful; if you want to find outfits featuring the Dior Book tote or Louis Vuitton Capucine bag, you can. Thousands of them.

You only need to look at the abundance of university courses that have been established since the early 2000s, based on varying fashion topics from business to marketing and fashion design, to know that people want to learn more, see more and do more with fashion. But mainly, they want to dress better and feel better, and it's because of the abundance of inspiration hitting their eyes every time they scroll.

Fashion is no longer an interest for a select few. It's been opened up, democratised and offered up to the audience on a plate. In previous years, you would only see the latest Chanel Cruise Collection images if you actively searched for them.

Christian Dior A/W17

Now, they're at the top of your newsfeed, gaining traction and being shared profusely — probably by you. The audience is hungry for the information, brand awareness is growing, bloggers are wearing the latest collections before they're even on the shelves and everyone else wants to buy into these brands that their favourite online star is wearing every day. It's an information and inspiration overload.

Even my mum, who has always liked fashion but not actively followed it or cared too much about brands and the industry, is trying new styles and outfits that she's seen others wearing online. People are experimenting more, finding their own style and learning about trends, collections, brands and the way the industry ticks without even actively searching for that information. Personally, I'm so pleased to see more people gain their confidence and find an interest in the way they present themselves. If my wearing a short dress can inspire someone to buy it and wear a short dress for the first time, and feel amazing, then hell yes for inspiration. Let's have more of it!

Where I look for fashion inspiration

Inspiration is everywhere. Like I said, you can't escape it. But when I really want to find it, I do a number of things:

1. If I'm just hoping to be inspired by new items and how to wear them, I often spend a few hours going through the new-in collections of all my favourite online stores. Or, if I'm in the city, I'll pop into their shops. Normally, you'll

quickly start spotting styles, shapes, fabrics or prints that overlap from store to store, so you can pick out the key pieces for the season.

2. Bloggers are popular for a reason – they're often very good at spotting the best items in the stores. I find myself popping over to my favourite blogs when I'm in a funk and need some inspo, just to see what they're wearing and how they're styling.

3. Magazines are my go-to when I'm travelling. On planes or trains, if I have no work to do, I love opening the pages of *Vogue*, *Elle* and *Porter* magazine to check out the brand adverts and shopping pages, as they are often filled with the latest items to hit the stores.

4. Online magazines are another way to find fashion-styling inspo. I especially love *Glamour* online, which I am very proud to have started writing a fashion column for in 2018, as well as *Marie Claire*, *Refinery29* and *Cosmo*. I just click through their latest fashion articles to see what's trending.

5. Instagram, of course, is daily inspiration. Scrolling through my feed, I like to save the images that show items I want to buy or styles I want to try.

6. Pinterest is another weekly place I like to visit, to see what their top pins are and what others might be loving right now. Making your own pinboards also helps, when you want to save particular outfits or pictures that you love to come back to later.

Be accessible and easy to find

Retail goes mobile

What was the last phone app you used? Instagram, Twitter, Notes, Calculator, Mail? Whatever you want to do, there's an app for it, and I hold my hands up in saying that I spend most of my life moving between about 10 apps on a daily basis.

When the iPhone app store was launched in July 2008, it was a space for games, social media apps and news sites. An assortment of 500 apps to kick-start what would become a rapidly growing hub of iPhone software. So rapidly growing that the number of apps now exceeds 2.8 million. The capabilities of our regular mobile phones got upgraded to the max and Internet efficiency enabled us to start using our phones on the go without having to wait 10 minutes for a webpage to load. It feels like a lifetime ago that the UK was upgraded to 4G in 2012, but now the idea that we used to survive on slow 3G

connections seems laughable. It was 3G and 4G capabilities
that catapulted ubiquitous mobile usage into the mainstream
and now ... well, we can buy anything we want from anywhere
we want, as long as we have a connection.

Over the three years when I was researching for my
PhD – focused on the app designs of our fave UK fashion
retailers – I spotted all of the updates, upgrades and newly
launched native mobile apps. Native apps are the ones you
download on the app store that have been built specifically by
the brand. It became a craze; every retailer needed one and
they were all jumping on board, one after another.

These native apps and responsive mobile websites became
more and more user-friendly as retailers started to realise just
how important they were to sales. Larger buttons, scrollable
images, one-click purchases and all that jazz. Just little tweaks
that helped the mobile customer to shop the same way they
would on a desktop, but in a handy, travel-sized format. The

experience got so handy that it now encourages 66 per cent of ASOS's customers to search and shop via their mobile. Very handy for ASOS, too.

While I was researching apps, I didn't realise just how quickly I would fall out of love with them. They were so useful, but now I find myself heading straight to my web browser and searching for a website instead. It's probably because I spend so much time on a desktop that I am used to shopping via a browser, and I'm in a habit of doing so. Perhaps I just need to give apps another chance, as it's probably been three years since I used a retail app to shop. Yet ASOS (always innovating) have launched a feature on their native app that enables users to buy now and pay later. It's only available via the app and will have acquired an entirely new audience for the brand. It's such a clever concept and a brilliant way to keep people coming back to the mobile app time and time again.

However, as long as the retailer has optimised their website to be responsive to mobile screens, they're likely to be benefiting from the huge waves of mobile traffic. Even for my blog, more than 50 per cent of my traffic is via mobile and tablets rather than a desktop computer. Brands had better make their mobile sites responsive, or their consumers won't be.

Be accessible and easy to find

My most-used apps and why they're amazing

Back when native apps were all the rage, I had app folders filled with my favourite high-street stores, so I could shop them on the go. But as I tend to use my browser for shopping instead these days, I thought I'd share the other apps that I use on my phone daily, and why they've become my go-to. I even checked my phone to see which were my most-used:

1. Instagram is number one, for obvious reasons. I'm almost embarrassed to say that 48 per cent of my battery life is spent on the 'gram in 24 hours. I can spend hours just scrolling the feed, gathering ideas and swooning over how cute my friends' dogs are.

2. Twitter is my place to read the news. I search through the latest trending stories and moments to catch up, and scroll the feed for a few minutes to see if I've missed anything happening in the blogging world.

3. Mail, of course. Every minute or so there's a new email popping up, so I can't escape it. I try to answer any emails as soon as they come in – I'm either proactive, or they will only be replied to the week after.

4. Lightroom CC is my go-to app for photo editing. It takes a bit of getting used to, but it allows for so much more control

over your imagery, colours and style. I tend to edit on my desktop, but I'm using the app more and more these days.

5.   WhatsApp is my way of keeping in contact with friends around the world. My best girlfriends are scattered across a few different continents, so we have a number of groups to allow us to continuously catch up.

6.   Camera, because the iPhone camera just keeps getting better and better. Who needs a DSLR anyway?

7.   Planoly is the app I use for planning out my Instagram feed. You can drag and drop your images around your picture board to create a faux feed, so you can check if your new photo will fit your aesthetic.

8.   YouTube is my everyday go-to for relaxation and time out. If I'm doing my make-up in the morning, cooking, sitting in the bath, I'll usually have a YouTube video playing in the background.

9.   Notes I use daily. Whether I'm coming up with ideas and need to write them down, or need to send a note to my desktop from my phone over iCloud, I'll write it into Notes and wait for it to appear on my other connected devices. I have Notes for most things going on in my life, to keep me organised.

10. Dropbox is my favourite for storage. My other half and I have one Dropbox between us that we throw work into when we need to ensure it's backed up. Plus, it's a great way to upload files from one device to another if your Airdrop isn't working or if your device isn't Apple.

Kate sells out the Burberry trench

The fashion world went crazy when they saw the Duchess of Cambridge, Kate Middleton, wearing that Reiss dress for her engagement photos, and the Polly Pushlock Mulberry handbag on a flight to Canada back in 2011. The items sold out in stores faster than the photographs could be printed. In the same year, the Burberry trench coat she wore sold out within hours, as did a £40 Topshop dress she wore back in 2007. This was before the days of Instagram, Pinterest and Twitter, when online news outlets, TV shows and magazines were the first to pick up stories and publish them.

Then we saw Meghan Markle, now the Duchess of Sussex, selling out the stock levels of Scottish accessories brand Strathberry in 2017 when she carried their tote to a charity event. The world once again saw the power of the Royals, and other influential faces, for selling out products in abundance. I was in the midst of designing my own collaboration collection with Strathberry when the images of Meghan broke. I was delighted. It sure did throw some more eyes onto a brand that I had loved for years.

Viral products are a phenomenon. An item suddenly picks up hype and goes out of stock overnight. A celebrity might wear it, a blogger might style it or a social star is paid to promote it. Suddenly the world and their mother own it and it becomes the most coveted item on the web. You may have noticed it happen in recent years with the popularity of the Chloé Faye handbag, Dior feminism T-shirts, Valentino Rockstuds, Supreme clothing, the Chanel Boy bag or a pair of Yeezy trainers. The more people wear it, the more people want it.

I remember the days of Von Dutch baseball hats, Rockport boots, Burberry baseball caps and Juicy Couture velour tracksuits – trends that exploded organically, even before the web, image-sharing sites or blogs. But now we're in a place where there are a multitude of platforms through which you can promote yourself and be noticed, and it takes just one significant moment, or a culmination of moments, to send a product into a viral frenzy.

Be accessible and easy to find

Kylie Jenner in Von Dutch

How to spot and buy a viral item

This is a tough one – a huge social star with 100 million followers could share a product and it may go out of stock within hours. In that case, you're out of luck unless you immediately google every retailer that might sell it. Use key words to describe the item you're looking for, and the chances are Google will find it in the images or shopping tabs.

Viral items are not just the products that sell out before you've even spotted them, though. Rather, they're the products that you see everywhere for a day or a week before they suddenly end up sold out in every store. Usually it's because the blogging and Instagram community have caught on to a particular trend. They're featuring it on their stories and Instagram feeds, so that product ends up going out of stock in a matter of days. That's certainly what happened for the Aquazzura Christy pumps in 2015, the double-G Gucci belt, the black Balenciaga Knife boots, the Dior bandeau bra with the contrast straps and the Dior T-shirts from the same line by Maria Grazia Chiuri. All of these products were all the rage until the point when you couldn't get your hands on them.

The best way to spot the items that are blowing up is to follow as many of the top fashion Instagrammers and bloggers as you can. If you start to notice one particular product appearing constantly during your scrolling, the chances are you're looking at a viral product.

Be accessible and easy to find

Michael Kors S/S13

Michael Kors is first to sponsor an Instagram ad

Can you even remember the days when you logged on to your social media account and it was only your friends' pictures that would show up in the feed? I remember reading articles suggesting that Facebook was eager to start monetising the platform – to take advantage of the billions of accounts that logged in every day. I was so disappointed. I knew it would mean advert after advert slotted in between Natalie's baby-scan photo and David's booze-cruise snaps, and I didn't want this friendly platform to change. But everything is different now. Nothing is free and you can't spend a minute online without seeing someone promoting something or other. I can't complain; as a blogger, I'm part of this issue.

Instagram teased its launch of advertisements for a number of weeks before slotting a Michael Kors advert into

the feeds of unsuspecting users in 2013. This was the first advert to ever appear on Instagram, and as with Facebook previously, it was met with mixed feelings. There was frustration towards Instagram rather than the Kors brand, but also anger from those that did not want their favourite social channel to become just as commercialised as the others. And yet, advertisements were here to stay.

For brands, the Instagram ad is just another marketing tool with which they can connect with a wide-reaching audience and Michael Kors was first in line to harness that power. The sponsored post is hated and admired in equal proportions, depending on who you speak to. It was only when the ASA (Advertising Standards Agency) took notice of the adverts being created within the growing YouTube space that they ruled that any paid-for content with editorial control must be marked as sponsored. And the #ad was born. The controversy gained speed when the media was quick to scapegoat Dan and

Phil, the YouTube stars turned radio presenters, for their Oreo advertisement video that displayed no mention of product promotion.

The practice of product promotions and advertisements within YouTube videos had been apparent for years, but no set rules had ever been stipulated and many adverts had gone under the radar. The #ad brought a tension to the YouTube community and an obvious dislike from the audience, although the product promotions in television and film had never created such a negative response. It seemed that the community didn't want their favourite YouTube channels to become too commercialised and ruled by the marketeers of the traditional world. Yet the #ad does not only apply to YouTube, with all other social channels having to follow in line. With the recent move to a more formal display of paid promotions on Instagram, with brands being tagged as a 'Paid Partnership', it seems that steps are in place to keep the collaborative movement going.

What do you think of ads? Are you sick of them in your feeds from brand promotions, or are you happy to see content creators collaborating with brands and publishing their own #ad content? Personally, I don't think the creator/brand relationship is going anywhere for quite some time. While a few naysayers are stating that the influencer market is dying, that seems like wishful thinking. Most of those who have a negative opinion of content creators are those who don't understand the industry, or who feel a threat to their own industry or role. People may need to adapt what they're doing to suit the changing audience, but there is room in this space for anyone and everyone who is making brilliant content, as there always has been.

#ad: How, why and when

The first ad I ever posted was in 2014. It was a YouTube video sponsored by L'Oréal for their world-famous Elnett hairspray. I'd been blogging for two years, and this sponsorship marked the start of something a little more exciting. Back then, disclaiming content as an ad was not a thing. You would mention it somewhere in the description box, and let your followers know that you had been paid to speak about that product, but the audience spoke very little about any concerns. It was just the way this fast-paced new industry was ticking along. Now, everything you post online must be disclaimed if it's paid for, and rightly so. The audience deserves to know if there may be some bias to your mention of that product. For anyone who posts sponsored content, or is hoping to in the future, I have a few thoughts on this:

Don't be bought

There are tens of thousands of retailers and brands out there who would love for you to talk about their products and would be willing to pay you to do so. If you don't use that product, or you don't like it, don't take the partnership. No matter what they're offering you, it's not worth lying to your followers about. I have turned down more money than I care to calculate, from brands that are not part of my current routines, whose policies I don't agree with, whose products are against my ethics or just aren't as good as another that I use. I always say, if I wouldn't recommend it to my mum, I won't recommend it to you. To do otherwise gives the industry a really bad name and reduces the trust for all of us.

Don't get pushed over

If you're going to start working with a company who are offering to pay you, ensure you have spoken with a professional concerning contracts. Trust me, you would not believe what can be written in the fine print. I almost signed away my personal image, for life, because the fine print looked pretty standard, when in fact it was far bigger than I realised. Protect yourself. You don't want to take a picture for a brand and find that image on the packaging of one of their products in a year's time, all because you signed something you didn't read. Your own brand or channels may be small now, but imagine if they grow to millions of followers. You don't want to be taken advantage of by a brand who thinks they can cash in on your success.

Don't get greedy

If you're a blogger working on a number of projects, try not to take on too much work. It can be easier said than done, as sometimes things pile up in the same week due to launch dates, but try to be mindful of it. Having a line-up of consecutive ads on your channels can be really damaging for your image and the trust your followers place in you. Choose the projects that mean the most to you, don't get greedy and be mindful of how you're appearing to the wider audience. And, if you're trying to hide the word 'ad' in your caption because you're ashamed of this collaboration, you absolutely shouldn't be doing it. Being paid to work with a huge brand is an amazing achievement. Own it!

RULE 2

Be aware of the impacts

Nothing gold can stay. While our ability to shop whenever we like, from wherever we like, is an amazing invention, there is always a drawback to our ubiquitous convenience. We all need to be more mindful of what our convenience is doing to the industry, as well as the planet. Luckily, the world is becoming more aware of the detrimental effects of extreme plastics usage and the requirement for sustainable fabrics and supply chains. It really is encouraging to see these environmental concerns being recognised, especially within the UK. But the consumer's desire for cheaper, faster alternatives and duplicates is killing the retail industry of the previous decades. It's a brand-new chapter; products are designed, developed and sold faster than ever before, the high street is struggling to keep up and everyone is in search of a bargain. So it begs the question: are we progressing or taking a few steps backwards? What can you do to reduce your own impact on the industry and the environment?

Death of the high street

I've become a thorough advocate for online shopping. Ever since I was at university and got totally hooked on it, I've always preferred to click the buy button and wait for my purchase to arrive. I just find it fuss-free and less frustrating than battling through crowds with a number of shopping bags.

But I'm under no illusion as to what this could mean for the future of retail. I remember the day when C&A was suddenly removed from the UK high street in May 2001, after years of being a favourite. And many other retailers have been pulled since, including BHS and Woolworths, if you remember those bags of pick 'n' mix. If everyone bought everything online (I'm looking at you specifically, Amazon), this trend would pick up more speed and the 'high street' as we know it could eventually die out. Thousands of small shopping streets and

individual stores all over the country have had to close over the past 10 years due to dwindling numbers of shoppers. People are pulled to the department stores, retail parks or to their favourite online site rather than their local shops, mainly due to discounts, sales and reduced prices online.

'Do you remember when we used to go to Tammy Girl, and you found that lilac handkerchief top that you had been searching for everywhere?' my mum asked me recently. And in my mind I was right back to the age of 12, on my monthly venture into Wigan town centre with Mum to buy something new for my wardrobe. We would make an afternoon of it, heading to our favourite café for a soup and sandwich as shopping fuel before spending hours in our favourite high-street stores.

Whenever I make the trip back to Wigan from London to see the family, me and Mum will still head out to our local retail park for a coffee and cake before walking around Next, M&S or George at Asda for a few treats for Mum. It's almost ingrained in us from years before. It's our bonding time, a little social affair for just me and her. But walking through the town centre of Wigan now, and the mall where Tammy Girl used to be (they all shut down in 2005), it's completely deserted. Hundreds of shops and cafés, completely gone.

Could such changes ever actually affect the biggest high streets around the globe? Locations like London's Regent Street, Chicago's Michigan Avenue or New York's 5th Avenue are gathering points for tourism, so I don't believe they would ever feel the loss of local trade in the same way. Shopping is a social occasion, for tourists, for locals and for family and friendship groups, and there will always be those people who prefer to try the clothes before they buy them. I usually only shop on the high street if I'm with a group of girlfriends or if I'm shopping last minute for a present, and I will always find time to shop in Selfridges if I have time to kill. But with retail giants such as Debenhams allegedly planning to close 10 of their 176 UK stores by 2022 due to the rise in purchases from their mobile site, maybe even the biggest high streets will see a few changes in their roster of stores.

It's no real surprise, is it? With such high overheads for rent, staff costs, lighting, logistics, stock and cleaning, it's no wonder that a multitude of brands have decided to remain specifically pure-play (online only). In the Manchester Arndale Centre, a small unit can supposedly cost £500,000 a year in rent alone. For a new brand starting out, or even a retailer who wishes to keep their overheads low, the online space is a much cheaper route to sales. So who can blame them for going digital?

Time to reflect

Think back to when you were aged 10 and answer the questions below in your head, or with your partner or friend, after you've read mine.

What was your favourite store?

It had to be Tammy Girl and Jane Norman, and I remember when a new Topshop store opened in Wigan when I was around 12 and it blew my mind!

Who did you usually go shopping with?

Usually with Mum, until I was in my teens, then my best mates Alison and Lucy and I would head into Wigan after school to raid Topshop's rails.

What's your favourite thing you ever bought at that age?

I had this white T-shirt that said 'Psycho Bitch' on the front. Hilarious. No idea what Mum was thinking when she let me buy that. I also remember buying an FCUK T-shirt back in the day that my grandad wasn't best pleased about.

What is your favourite store now?

I would say my favourite store now is Selfridges, but if I had to choose an actual brand, then Me + Em is my current favourite.

Do you prefer to shop online or offline?

Online, unless I'm with my girlfriends, in which case I'd prefer to be out shopping, drinking coffee in between shops and catching up.

Why do you, or do you not, prefer online shopping?

You can see the entire collection much faster than you can see everything in store. You can see more styling ideas, ways to wear it and, depending on how advanced the site is, how that item moves and drapes in a catwalk view. You can also get it delivered to your door, usually via next-day delivery, and send it back just as easily, which means you don't have to struggle carrying bags around busy London all day. I think if I lived in Manchester again, I'd love shopping physically so much more!

Fast fashion piles up

Have you seen the Netflix documentary *The True Cost*? It's an incredible insight into this industry, the appalling practices that go on behind the scenes and the real effects of fast-fashion shopping. As a blogger, I am extremely conscious that I walk the line of ultra-materialism daily; let's be serious, blogging is an industry built on reviewing, informing and inevitably inspiring people to buy one product over another. And yet, morally, I hope that my followers don't buy items they don't need, in the abundance that I have to. I buy a lot of new items for my content – to style new outfits for photographs and to display new trends and styles in haul videos on my YouTube channel – because my audience is looking for fashion and beauty inspiration constantly. A lot of those products I send back after I've offered styling advice and trend ideas to my audience, so my intake is actually

nowhere near what it seems. But I would never intend for my audience to buy the entire collection of clothes I have bought – it's excessive and completely unnecessary. If I wasn't a blogger, I would make much more minimal choices regarding how many new fashion items I add to my wardrobe. So I can openly admit that the birth of the YouTube haul, and fashion blogging in general, is a big part of our excess fashion waste problems.

But if there were no new items to show every week or fortnight, the trend to show more and more wouldn't be so prevalent. This quick turnaround and continuous stream of new products to buy and buy and buy has likely been accelerated by the fast-fashion retailers. One could point the finger at Primark's shockingly low prices, or the likes of lower-priced online stores such as Boohoo, Fashionnova, In the Style or PrettyLittleThing. They're affordable, on-trend and offer the perfect items to wear for a night on the town. When Primark opened its biggest worldwide store in Manchester in October 2001, the city thought all its Christmases had come early. But as fast as the retailer was bringing cheap stock into store or uploading items to site, their avid shoppers were eating them up, throwing them onto a 'used pile' and buying a new one for next weekend. They can, because they're so affordable, so why wouldn't they?

Herein lies our problem. Affordability often equals frivolity, bad purchase decisions, clothing worn only once and a huge pile-up of unwanted fabrics lying on trash heaps. And it's only getting worse. If you haven't already, watch the documentary I mentioned above, as it summarises the enormous issues far better than I can bullet-point them, and they require so much more attention than that. But making better clothing purchase decisions is something that everyone should be looking to do, myself included.

Ways to purchase more ethically

1. Don't hit the buy button unless you've decided that you really need it in your collection.

2. Ask yourself if you have any similar items, and therefore if you need to also buy this one.

3. Is this product of a good-enough quality that you will be able to use it for a number of years, or at least a good number of wears?

4. Is this retailer likely to have used ethical practices to source and manufacture this garment at such a fast turnaround and in such quantities?

5. For the same cost per wear, could you find something similar online from another retailer that is of a higher quality and may last you longer?

6. If you still want the item, try it on at home and then make the decision as to whether it's a necessary purchase. Be sure to send it back if it's not – don't just leave it in the bag and forget to return it within the 28-day return period.

Be aware of the impacts

Karl Lagerfeld

Continuous sales are killing seasonal trends

As Karl Lagerfeld huddled models and press onto green buses towards St Germain from Place de la Concorde in May 2005, his guests did not anticipate that they were headed towards Café de Flore to watch the Chanel Resort Collection over champagne and canapés. They were treated to a fashion show along the way: tweeds, sequins and Parisian monuments cut into fabrics, followed by a full evening display of silk and chiffon gowns and red-carpet glamour when they reached the French café.

Around a similar time, various other fashion houses were displaying their own cruise, holiday or resort collections, as they are interchangeably known, adding another runway show to their roster and offering a new line of 'holiday appropriate' clothing to their stores. Or at least that's how they started decades ago. The initial premise of the resort collection was to offer wealthy ladies a line of clothing to suit their warm holidays in the winter months. But in recent years, designers have admitted that resort collections are not about holiday wear at all. In the current age of constant press, social media, celebrity dressing and continuous purchasing, designers create cruise collections to take their customers from October to early spring, freshening up the stores with new products to continue interest, keep customers coming back before the new-season wear drops and ensure they have new items to dress their favourite celebrities.

And so, two seasons and two catwalk shows a year became four with cruise and then pre-fall. An additional two haute-couture shows equals six, and the inclusion of menswear takes the number of shows to eight. It is no wonder that trends have become diluted and sporadic with the constant insertion of new products every two months.

Cara Delevingne (left) and Kendall Jenner

Christian Dior A/W17

One could argue that there are not necessarily key trends or colours at this point either; rather, key pieces for every few months, followed by the next exciting item that is seen at the catwalk show halfway through the year. Such movement of stock and additions of new product lines are inevitably what ramped up the need for store sales over the last decade. Gone are the days of the Boxing Day sale and summer sale, creating havoc as people lined up to rush inside the store for a first pick of the discounted rails. We see online adverts for mid-season sales consistently throughout the year, as each retailer is begging for attention in an industry that is pumping out collections faster than the consumer can devour them. At least the retailers now have customer incentives to sell their latest sale stock, sending out emails to their customers, reminding them of further markdowns and offering extra discounts on particular collections when you order online. The online customer always wants more and in the fastest way possible, so perhaps it's the shopping habits of the online consumer that has increased the requirement of continuous products and thus continuous sales? Either way, we all just need to chill a little.

It comes down to this: with the continuous push of new collections and the requirement for amplified sales throughout the year, seasonal trends are dying. Who needed sock boots, tiny sunglasses or oversized padded jackets anyway?

Be aware of the impacts

My sale shopping tips

I have never been a big sale-shopping gal. I hate the idea of fighting over products that have been thrown carelessly onto rails, as though they have lost all value and just need to be flogged. Which is why I like to shop online for sales – at least then I can't see if the items are coming out of a big, chaotic box of stock. I can imagine they were taken off the shop floor by a person wearing white gloves, dusted, placed into a bag and neatly shipped to me. The shopping queen inside me can dream.

But there are times when I do splurge on luxury online sales, so I thought I'd pass on my tips:

- If the item goes into the sale and it's the exact product you've always wanted and dreamed of, and you have nothing like it in your collection, but it was previously out of your price limit, buy it. No questions asked.

- If the item goes into the sale and it's the product you loved but in a different material or colour, ask yourself which outfits you could wear it with. Is it appropriate for the season or the season coming up next? If not, you know you won't wear it, and by the time the next season comes around, you'll have lost that love for it. If it is, and you can wear it with lots of outfits, buy it. Check the refund policy first, but in most cases you can always send it back later if you decide it's not right.

- If it's something you spot in the sale and you've never seen it before, do the same as before. What could you wear it with? What events do you have coming up that you'd wear it for? Why is this product special to you? You could always buy it now, try it on at home and see if you love the quality and style in person (again, depending on the refund policy).

- Just because the price is a lot lower does not mean you need it or should buy it. You need to think about how useful or necessary it will be with your current wardrobe, or future wardrobe if it's a big, big splurge. If it's a Chanel bag and it happens to be discounted by 20 per cent, yes, it's a lot of money off, but it's also still a lot of money. In that case, if you're in store and falling for a bag but you're not sure, ask them to hold it for you for an hour or so, go for a coffee, and if you cannot wait to get back to the store to have it, then it's meant to be. If you're really not that bothered, don't buy it.

October 2011

Siri is stalking our shopping habits

'What can I help you with?' asks Siri to every iPhone user in
the world. That's over 700 million people. For those users who
have activated Siri knowingly or unknowingly, she listens to their
every word. She's meant to; she's supposed to be on hand for
whenever she is needed and therefore she is always listening.
And while Apple have stated that they won't ever share
anything that Siri hears with anyone, it begs the question:
where is that data going? (You can turn off Siri in Settings, so
don't panic.)

But it's not just Apple's Siri, Amazon's Alexa, Microsoft's
Cortana and Google Assistant that are listening, watching and
tracking our every move. Online marketing, email marketing,
social adverts and YouTube ads are all targeting the consumer
everywhere they move online. That time you went onto Net-A-

Porter to find a pair of Valentino heels, no doubt you then saw them in every online banner advert for the next few weeks. Or when you shopped on an international site and later received adverts with delivery or discount codes to incentivise you to shop again. Or when you filled your online shopping bag with five items and they suddenly ended up in your inbox with a subject titled, 'Did you forget something?' ... No, I did not, but thank you for reminding me that I'm broke this month, and that you're practically stalking me.

If we don't see a clothing item in our email inbox to entice us to buy, we see it in blog advertisements, Instagram ads and our Facebook feed. Fashion brands are willing our subconscious to take the plunge and make that purchase we had thought better of the day before. It's a little nudge here and a little nudge there.

A mere chat with a friend about the latest Chanel perfume could lead to the appearance of the Chanel advert on your Instagram feed hours later, or so people say. While Facebook has denied that they use conversations to tailor advertisements, many people have remained dubious. When I recently asked a friend where her t-shirt was from, she replied 'Anine Bing', a brand I had somehow never heard of or searched online for before. The next day I was served an Anine Bing instagram ad on my feed. I'm sceptical.

So it would seem that eyes and ears are everywhere, especially when it comes to our shopping and spending habits. Brands don't want us to abandon our shopping bag, so they will keep on reminding us how fabulous we might look if we just took the plunge and bought it.

How to protect your shopping habits

1. If you don't want to allow your phone to listen to your conversations, just in case you say 'Siri', or 'Hey, Google', turn off these features. You won't be able to use Siri any more, but did you ever use it in the first place?

2. If you really don't want to be targeted with email marketing after you've been privately shopping, be sure that you're not logged in to your account on that retailer's website. If they don't know it's your account, they can't email you about the products later.

3. Take the time to unsubscribe from store emails that are tempting you in. If you find yourself heading onto the Harrods website every time they email you the latest collection, it's time to get unsubscribed. Just scroll to the bottom of the email and find that tiny 'unsubscribe' button.

4. Go incognito. While you're on Google Chrome, press the command, shift and N keys together to open up a private page that won't show up in your history and won't remain tracked on your computer. That way, your habits can't be followed after you've exited that page.

Wear it once, resell it tomorrow

Oh, how I remember those days of selling items on eBay! I had an old pair of beaten-up jeans that I thought someone, somewhere, might be willing to buy, so I stuck them on eBay alongside a number of other used and pretty worn-out items. I was at university and it seemed like a fantastic way of profiting from my used wardrobe for extra Friday-night drinking funds. But my goodness was it frustrating. Buyers wouldn't pay, they'd want a refund, they'd complain about anything to reduce charges, and posting lots of items at one time would be a total mission. After the first time I tried it, I thought no more. eBay launched in 1995 as a marketplace for any possible item – cars, cameras, electricals – but clothing not so much, unless it's really vintage and pretty darn special. Sure, Nasty Gal and Sézane both had to start somewhere, but I bet they're glad they've found their own private space now, away from the chaos.

Thankfully, with online growth came a number of new selling platforms specifically made for fashion buyers and sellers. Depop launched into the world in 2013, a simple phone app where you can upload your items – usually fashion, but it doesn't have to be – onto your own selling page with pictures you took on your smartphone. If you upload enough times, you can amass an audience who will be there for the next time you upload. I've sold hundreds of used fashion items on Depop over the years, and it really is super hassle-free. And while this isn't a #ad for Depop, I think their easy approach to selling is probably why the fashion recycling and selling culture has become so huge.

You wear that dress one time for a Saturday night out, and the next day you could have it up on Depop for someone else's Saturday night. As fast as you bought it, you can have it folded, packaged and shipped off to your buyer. And so fashion is being recycled more than ever before. It's a great thing in a shopping environment where £1 T-shirts can be bought from huge retailers and thrown into a bin as soon as they've been worn once. Instead, charity shops are receiving more clothing donations, reselling sites such as Depop and eBay are thriving from recycled clothing and even the luxury space has managed to cash in.

Vestiaire Collective and Rebelle are just two online brands that have grown and thrived from the reselling trend. The designer bag collector can sell their latest purchase to a luxury adorer somewhere else in the world, vetted and procured via Vestiaire's teams. That Dior bag that was perfect for last season's outfits can now be uploaded online, in a luxury marketplace, ready for another Dior fan to eat it up – only at a marginally reduced price, but still, everyone loves a bit of a discount, right?

What to do with your used items

○ If it's in good-enough condition and someone else would probably want to wear it, stick it on Depop and make yourself a little bit of cash back from the original price. It's better in someone else's wardrobe than in yours, picking up dust.

○ If it's not clothing or beauty based, eBay is probably your best bet. It's a site that still has a huge audience – people are still searching there for everything that's ever existed in the world.

○ For luxury bags and shoes, give Depop a try first. It's not the luxury buyers' market, but you may find the odd luxury lover who is searching for a bargain Chanel bag that you've fallen out of love with. If you find luxury hard to sell there, try Vestiaire or Rebelle. With their VIP services, you can send off your designer items to their offices to be photographed, listed and sold without you having to lift a finger.

- If you want to sell beauty products that are still within date but unused, again I would recommend Depop. There are a variety of buyers on there who may be interested in designer make-up at a more affordable price.

- If you're someone who isn't up for the hassle of reselling but you also realise that throwing clothing in the bin isn't the most sustainable option, then why not donate to your local charity shop? I send my clothes to the British Heart Foundation every few months. They have a really useful pick-up service if you give your local store a ring, or you could take the bags in yourself. At least then your old clothes can profit a charity, rather than ending up in a trash heap.

- Finally, what about organising a clothes swap? You can always rely on friends and family to have something in their wardrobe that you love, and vice versa. Clothes swaps mean you can shift items you no longer wear, guilt-free, and find something in your friend's wardrobe to replace them with.

Alexander Wang sues the counterfeits

It's 2016 and Wang just won a $90-million legal battle against 459 websites selling counterfeit versions of his products. Of course, he will never actually receive all that cash – the 50 defendants behind the 459 websites selling fake Wang goods will probably never be found, but even if they were, they could never afford to pay such a fee. It's more a statement to the world that counterfeiting is a pretty serious deal.

I'm sure we've all strolled along the boardwalk of a sunshine resort and passed by a handful of sellers with Chanel and Dior bags lined up on a dusty rag on the floor. I was actually bought one once from China by an ex-boyfriend's grandad, and although I was grateful for the surprise gift, I knew I could never wear it. It felt completely wrong, fake and unfair. Like I would be ripping off the brand myself by flaunting it around.

Unfortunately, though, the world of fake goods, counterfeits and imitations has only grown over the last 15 years, especially with the rise in Internet sellers and fake sites. eBay is rife with inauthentic products and even some of the biggest luxury reselling websites have countless negative reviews of fake goods being sold as genuine items. The fakes are now so good that even the genuine luxury sellers can't spot the difference!

Whenever I think of fake items doing the rounds, no story springs to mind faster than Burberry. Back in 2004, when 'chavs', 'scallies', 'townies' or whatever your town branded them, were walking around in their tracksuit bottoms and Burberry baseball caps, it marked a serious demise for the Burberry brand. Burberry had become so globally ubiquitous that everyone wanted in on the action – just not with the same price tag. With the brand having become negatively associated with the 'chav' culture, as the tabloids coined it, the average UK Burberry customer no longer wanted to be seen

wearing its genuine items. UK sales hugely declined, and it took a number of years for the brand to regain its luxury footing. Luckily, in 2008 they were back on a pedestal again as one of the top five revenue-generating brands in the world, but for any other brand, it could have marked the end of their customer base altogether.

But it's not just counterfeits ruining brand image and value any more. The speed with which online retailers can imitate and churn out duplicate goods that resemble those on the catwalks means you can buy a pair of shoes from your favourite online or high-street retailer that look almost identical to those beautiful new Balenciagas. Public Desire especially has become known as the online store to visit if you want to find a pair of shoes that are a near-enough copy of the luxury counterpart. The other day I spotted a pair of Balenciaga duplicates over on the Topshop website, too. They don't have the brand name anywhere on the items, and they have a number of changes to the shoes to make them fair to sell, but the likeness is uncanny.

What does this mean for luxury stores? There will always be customers who prefer to buy into a designer brand, mainly to feel as though they are part of something; part of a group of people who own this genuine product, designed by one of their favourite Creative Directors, or sold by a brand they adore or aspire to. That is certainly how I feel about buying luxury items and, even if an imitation looks identical, I'd rather own the real thing. Counterfeiting is a different ball game, in that the fakes are made to look authentic, carrying the brand's logos and emblems, and they're sold on the premise that they're genuine – taking a consumer away from buying the brand's authentic product. It's a black market and, as we have seen before with the Burberry case, the potential to ruin a brand's image, customer base and market share is huge.

The best places to find the designer dupes

Now I'm not talking rip-offs, but items that are super-similar in style to the item you might be looking for . . .

Shoes: Public Desire, Topshop, Zara, H&M

Bags: Zara, Topshop, Primark, Missguided

Clothing: Mango, Ducie London, ASOS, SheIn, Missguided

RULE 3

Be social

We're living in an age where social interactions have gone crazy. People have more friends online than they do offline, and everyone knows where you are, who you're with, what you're wearing and what you're eating, at all hours of the day. Our social channels are counting on us being sociable; they reward those who publish more, engage more and spend extra time on the platform. It's a big cyclical chain of 'I'll scratch your back if you scratch mine', or rather, 'I'll like your pic, if you like mine.' So, make sure your social space is somewhere you want to be. Follow the people who inspire you and unfollow the ones that make you unhappy. People everywhere are creating content for your inspiration, entertainment and enjoyment, so take it for what it is.

It's surprising how long it's taken some retailers to catch on to the requirement for true social interaction. Having an up-to-date, informative and inspirational social channel is much more essential than some seem to realise. For those that are growing their social game personally or professionally, it's about learning how to do it most effectively for the ever-changing followers' wants and needs. For those out of the loop and jumping in for the first time, it's about getting prepared to join a brand-new world.

The fashion blogging evolution

When I was around eight, I was playing on this huge lump of a computer in our spare room at home. It was around 1997, Dad had bought us a desktop computer for the first time and I can't explain my elation. It didn't work all that well, but it could manage to complete the odd time-wasting task, so I was thrilled. I easily spent the most time out of everyone in the household staring into the enormous screen every day, playing games and surfing what there was of the web back then. And it was around that time that I discovered a site that allowed you to design your own website. It was clunky and hard to use, but I spent hours online, building my own space where I would share images, thoughts and lyrics from my favourite songs. It was building that website at such a young age that formed my love for sharing, designing and developing online.

This enjoyment only grew in the days of Myspace, when the majority of kids were using code to develop their Myspace page into something unique. Everyone just picked it up as they went along, so hundreds of kids, including me, were teaching themselves coding hacks at 16 or younger. Myspace hinted at a desire for people to have their own unique account of themselves online for others to view and follow. Hence why we were all automatically friends with Myspace Tom without even knowing who he was.

It was around 2006 when fashion blogs began to surface. They were an entirely new platform, offering personal opinions, style advice and reviews from the ordinary girl in the street to the interested reader. It was a portal of information, an online reading book for one inspired person to pass on to the next inspired reader. It created light relief from the corporate advertising techniques and traditional marketing methods that every brand had exhausted for decades, and suddenly the most normal of people were becoming more popular.

The first fashion bloggers succeeded in creating a name for themselves in a very open and unexplored arena. Just think of how quickly names like Perez Hilton grew to fame, after being one of the first celebrity and fashion gossip bloggers in the world. Garance Doré started her blog in 2006 and soon became one of the most respected writers in the industry, later publishing her book, *Love, Style, Life,* as well as a podcast for the fashion savvy and turning her blog into a style studio for various writers. Scott Schuman also deserves recognition as the godfather of street-style photography, being one of the first to take to the streets of New York to document the local styles in September 2005. He too has published his own books,

Garance Doré

Scott Schuman

selling hundreds of thousands of copies worldwide, and working with various brands on campaign shoots and projects. And then there is Susie Bubble, who became the poster girl for UK fashion bloggers and the press back in 2006. The space was somewhat empty and, at that time, mainly just a hobby for those who wanted to write and share. But as the years rolled on, it inspired hundreds and then thousands to follow in the footsteps of the innovators. Right up until the point where, now, the space is extremely saturated.

Blogging started as a hobby for me, too. I thought full-time blogging was a mythical and juvenile pipe dream. It was only 18 months into my own blogging journey that everything began to change in the online social space and bloggers started to take on the mainstream world. Fashion and beauty industries really started to take notice. Emails would flood my inbox from brands offering to send me a product from their latest collection; a new bag from their range, their latest heels or the most coveted dress on their site. Or I could choose my own favourite products from their collection and they would send them over to my flat in Manchester.

It was a new world for both blogger and brand. Previously, the fashion editors of the most coveted magazines would be the ones to feature the newest apparel and wear the latest styles to attend the runway shows. This new form of blogger relationship seemed to speed up the process, often enabling a brand's new item to be featured on a fashion blog or social channels that very afternoon. And as fashion bloggers became more popular with engaged and loyal audiences, brands stood back and gasped as they saw that products featured once by a blogger were sold out the following day. The fashion blogger became a direct route to an active audience.

By 2017, the Internet was filled with hundreds of bloggers, managing to maintain their blog full-time without any other means of income. Over the years, blogging became a viable job opportunity for those who had dared to dream in the beginning. To a certain extent, the industry is very much the same now as it was in 2014. Brands offer products to bloggers to be featured in their latest style posts and Instagrams. Only now, bloggers are wiser and more business savvy; they know what is at stake. Especially for those who have grown their following to the size of a small country, featuring a brand's new product and key message comes at a price. And rightly so. *Vogue* doesn't give away free advertising space, and neither should anyone else. Blogging became more than just a hobby within a very short

space of time, forcing many bloggers to start running their own brands and limited companies and creating their own business strategies.

With the evolution of blogging came the change in fashion. Fashion blogs, Tumblr profiles and Lookbook.nu opened up the fashion world to so many more eyes than ever before. Pre-blogging, the fashion industry could be quite alienating, elitist and model-focused. The trends were created by one, watched by a selective few and picked up by the majority of retailers to sell to the masses. Those who didn't follow fashion avidly would pick up an item in their local store and wear it in the way they may have seen on the in-store mannequin or their favourite TV show. This new form of fashion media brought with it bundles of inspiration; the everyday person wearing clothing in inspiring but wearable outfits, offering their views and advice on products and creating an aspirational lifestyle. It heightened the accessibility of fashion information and styling advice for the average person, and enabled the online fashion retailers to thrive. More fashion inspiration leads to more fashion purchases. And with the reader already online, viewing all of this information and inspiration, the next easy step is to click 'buy' in their shopping cart. Bloggers were the fashion retailers' wildest dream.

But what's next? The depleting number of readers tuning into blogs and magazines online, but the growth in video watch times, would signify a preference for easy, digestible video usage over text. Yet there will always be those who prefer to read – whether it's a hardback book, a magazine, a newspaper or these pages you're holding now. There will just be fewer blogs, fewer online pages that thrive and a focus on higher-quality content.

How to start your own blog

Though saturated, this industry still has room for everyone and anyone. Every person is unique and they can create and bring their own personal ideas to the fashion table. They just have to be good, original and high-quality ideas. Whether that's in their styling, their creation of imagery or their writing style; some bloggers are being made overnight due to a viral image or a shared article. Something that grabs everyone's attention. Anyone can do it, and there's still so much to play for. So what do you need to do to start?

1. Choose a name for your blog

Whether that's your own name or a brand name. For example, Inthefrow, Cupcakes and Cashmere or Song of Style. When you've chosen that name, see if you can get the social handles to match. I only settled on Inthefrow because I was able to choose @inthefrow on every single social channel, so that everything matched. It just helps, when someone is searching for you, to keep everything succinct.

Also, be sure that your chosen name is available as a domain. For example, inthefrow.com. I would recommend .com as the suffix, only because it's the most common, but you could also buy .co.uk or .london. If it's available, buy it. There are lots of sites that help you buy a domain, just type in the phrase 'buy the domain for yournewblogname.com' into Google and a plethora of sites will want to help you. It will probably cost you between £5–10 a year, so even if you decide you don't want to blog after a month, you haven't really lost out. But it then means that you own your domain and every social channel under that same name. Nice and organised.

2. Get designing

The best blogs are those that have really thought about how the audience would want to navigate around the site and how aesthetically beautiful it is. One of the reasons my blog grew when I first started it was because I had put time and effort into the design. If it's great to look at, and easy to read, it's much easier to draw in new readers. I designed three versions of inthefrow.com myself before asking for development help from an awesome blog design store named Pipdig. I gave them my designs and they whipped up my blog into something that looks pretty great!

3. Spend time on your content

It's all about high-quality content now, with beautiful imagery, great writing and something that your audience can learn and take away from their time on the page. So take the greatest shots and work on your writing to make it interesting and worth returning for.

4. Be consistent with your posts

When I started, I posted daily, sometimes twice daily. I was trying to get my blog out there and to build up a backlog of posts that would show up on Google. I was absolutely obsessed with posting, so I couldn't wait to hit publish on the next post, and then the next. However often you choose to post, stay consistent. Once a week, twice a week or every day. Give your readers something to come back for, at a certain time.

5. Put yourself out there on social media

Twitter is great for sharing your links and images from your blog posts – and be sure to tag the brands you mention. Instagram is another useful tool for sharing your blog and images, and for tagging brands. Be sure to have your blog linked in the profile of your Instagram page, too. Chat with other bloggers to make friends in the community, on every social channel, and over time it will help you to get your blog out there. Commenting on other blogs can also help.

6. For any additional help

I've written a lot of different posts about growth and building a blog audience on my actual blog, inthefrow.com.

Be social

The world gets hashtagged

#Barcamp. Believe it or not, that was the first ever hashtag posted on Twitter in August 2007 by Chris Messina. I won't pretend to know what 'barcamp' means, but this word, and more importantly the hashtag in front of it, is one of the most important moments in Internet history. When was the last time you used a hashtag? I use hashtags almost daily on most of my social channels, whether I'm grouping my imagery into #fashionblogger photos, my outfits into #OOTD groups or my bag into the #diorbag page. I don't even think about it, and I never questioned where it came from. As far as I was concerned, it was just a way of tagging your content into a thread of other similar content, with the same hashtag, so that users could find it. But the consequences of this are huge, and for none more so than the fashion industry.

Finding, searching, researching and inspiring has never been easier than it is right now. Hashtags are a simple grouping and filtering system, collecting every person's content together with the same hashtag, forming a feed related to that one and only topic. Of course, you'll get a rogue, random image thrown into the mix by someone tagging their photo wrongly, often on purpose, but in the majority of cases you can filter the millions of images posted per day into one concise group. So, so clever, hey?

If you're searching for Balenciaga boot inspo, you only need to search the #Balenciagaboots feed to find a plethora of images that suit your needs. Or #Tiffanyring or #Yeezys or any other item or brand you want to stalk. There are over 3 million images of styling ideas, flatlays and outfit inspo hashtagged specifically for the #ChanelBoyBag and over 2 million for the #HermesBirkin – just in case you needed any more excuses to buy one. I, too, have fallen into the black hole of a handbag hashtag feed and found myself heading to the store the next day to buy one. And so, the fashion world is linked together, one hashtag, one item and one trend at a time. For fashion designers, bloggers, retailers and shoppers, it's never been easier to promote, inspire and be inspired.

It all started over on Twitter in 2007, but it was October 2010 and the launch of Instagram that changed the fashion space entirely. There, we are continuously shown the perfect lifestyles, the most popular brands, the latest trends and the coolest outfits, all encouraging more and more impulsive purchases and general spending. Social superstars are being made from behind a mobile camera lens and their reach, combined with what they're wearing, make their pages an advertiser's dream. Marketing budgets are increasingly being spent on Instagram-worthy content and glamorous trips to the Hamptons rather than on traditional billboards, magazine adverts and even online banners. This one social platform is hugely responsible for switching the focus from traditional media to digital.

With at least one in three people having bought an item they have seen on Instagram, and with more than 1 billion active users in 2018, Instagram has turned into one of the most successful advertising spaces ever created. And it is the hashtag that glues the whole social world together.

10 hashtags and tips you should use for your fashion photos

1. #ootd

2. #outfit

3. #instastyle

4. #fashionblogger

5. #fashioninspo

6. #style

7. Find a fashion account that shares other people's photos and use their particular hashtag – often located in their profile bio.

8. Hashtag the brands you're wearing – for example, #chanel, #maxmara, #asos, etc.

Giambattista Valli S/S17

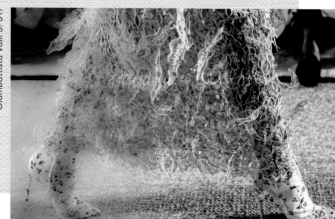

Victoria Beckham S/S18

9. Hashtag the item, if it´s particularly famous – #Birkin, for instance, or #sockboots, #lvcapucine, #ladydior, etc.

10. Look out for popular style hashtags used by big accounts or even brands. The Revolve hashtag, #Revolvearoundtheworld, is meant to be used if you´re wearing anything from Revolve, but ensures you get into that popular feed of images. The same goes for #babesofmissguided and #asseenonme for ASOS. Take advantage of getting into bigger image feeds.

Fashion Pinspiration for the masses

Hands up who has a wedding-inspiration Pinterest board? Be honest, even if you´ve made it secret so your other half won´t think you´re wedding obsessed. The majority of girls I know all have a Pinterest board for their future/upcoming/past wedding – hell, most have a multitude! One board for hairstyle ideas, another for table settings, locations, dresses, rings, photographers – you can practically plan your whole wedding before you even have a partner! And that´s what makes Pinterest so absolutely addictive: curating, planning, organising and pinning into beautifully themed virtual pin-boards.

While Pinterest claim they are not a social platform for person-to-person interaction, they certainly enable an interaction between product and consumer that has never been seen before. Their launch in March 2010 led to a product- and image-sharing frenzy, with users eager to curate their own visual themes on unique, shareable pin-boards. It's the wedding planner's dream and the scrapbook for the interior decorator; the foodie lover's sanctuary of recipes and the fashion girl's haven for style tips – the ultimate place for inspiration when it comes to visual imagery, curating and planning.

And while consumers and pinning lovers are mad about it, it's also a place for brands to pull together collections and inspiration. Why not target this pinning-fanatic consumer, as well as the tweeting, Instagram-adoring YouTube watcher? Pinterest has 2 billion search queries a month and 200 million monthly active users. It's a goldmine! Of course, brands wanted to take advantage, and Pinterest were happy to oblige by bringing in advertising slots. Now the user can search for visual images for their wedding, but also have ideas handed to them in advertisement form. I guess it's a win-win for everyone, especially Pinterest.

Top tips for perfect pinning

1. Create as many boards as you like. You can't really have too many, but having defined themes to each keeps them user-friendly and will encourage others to follow along. If you make your boards a confusing mess of random imagery, no one is going to want to follow you and see what you pin next.

2. Use keywords and hashtags in your captions. Pinterest works best with keywords, as other users will often search

for long, specific phrases. If your photo is a picture of you with long, brown, curly hair, name it as such, as it's likely that someone might search for that phrase or similar. Almost tell Pinterest exactly what is in the image – it can't see your photo, it can only read about it, so make it easier to find and add into relevant search feeds.

3. Make your board names easy to find and completely relevant. Spell them correctly, not with spaces between each letter to look all pretty, or with emojis or symbols to make them all fancy. Pinterest can't read those in the same way and so your boards won't be shared with other users in the same way. Make your titles clear and straight to the point.

4. Keep your page looking aesthetically pleasing. If someone finds it, give them a reason to follow you or re-pin your images. They're more likely to love what you're doing on Pinterest if you've shown a lot of love to the overall design and direction of your whole page.

5. Link to your website, if you have one. Again, why not have anyone who finds your Pinterest page also find your website, and click through!

6. If you do have a website or a blog, pin all of your best imagery. The kind of imagery that you feel others may like to share, too. Pin it straight from your blog and don't change the URL in the options, so that when other users click through, they're met with your website, increasing your blog traffic and encouraging new users, and returning readers, to your site.

Vogue starts a social shopping trend

It's midnight and I'm scrolling Facebook to see which old high-school friend has just had another baby. And while I'm here, I might as well click the link to the Net-A-Porter page for the pretty YSL handbag they just promoted. Why not? It's fast, simple and there's no harm in window shopping. Or hitting the 'buy' button ten minutes later.

Social shopping – it's the modern way to purchase, didn't you know? Clickable images on Pinterest take you right to the source of the product you love. You can like an image on Instagram and the links to buy the products can be sent directly to your email. In fact, one night in April 2018, I saw an Instagram advert with clickable links on the actual image for the first time. If you wish to find out about the latest styles from your favourite retailer, you can head over to your Facebook feed, or why not scour the latest 20 per cent discounts from a retailer you follow on Twitter? Anywhere you socialise, you can also purchase.

On the set of
Dolce & Gabbana
campaign shoot

But it was *Vogue* magazine back in 2010 who were first to break the social-shopping mould. Their first-of-its-kind iPad app came complete with the digital version of the magazine, offering clickable links to the products displayed in the pictures. You could fall in love with a dress in a Dolce & Gabbana advert and be led directly to the product page for an immediate purchase. The consumer and their wardrobe became more connected than ever before. What could be easier than spotting an item of clothing or a pair of shoes that you love, and buying it directly from that page? Especially if that page is somewhere that you spend the majority of your time online anyway.

This was Facebook's thinking when they incorporated stores into the social network and enabled users to buy directly through Facebook. No one would ever have to leave the platform again! Or so they hoped. This idea swept into Pinterest with shoppable images that directed you straight to the product pages. And with Instagram stories and the 'swipe up' feature for verified users, consumers could see and buy an item directly from an Instagram story. The easier the route to purchase, the better for the retailer.

And with new technologies come even more routes to shop. RewardStyle, a web tool used by bloggers to help monetise content, were first to devise the 'Like to know it' app, enabling an Instagram user to like a photo of an outfit and have the product links sent directly to their email. We are at a point where you can literally 'like' to shop. And in the future we will likely reach a place where every image anywhere online can be shopped by anyone. With billions of people now connected to a social network from every corner of the world, the implications for the fashion industry and those working within it are unfathomable.

The brands to follow on social

Here's a list of who I'd recommend you to follow if you're looking for some fashion inspo on your favourite feeds. Three brands on each platform, all of which keep their channels up to date, are always posting creative or image-based content, often with direct links to the items they show, and continue to keep their branding succinct.

- Twitter: @chanel, @topshop, @netaporter
- Facebook: @burberry, @tedbaker, @levis
- Instagram: @dior, @revolve, @gianvitorossi
- YouTube: Net-A-Porter, Amazon, Nike
- Pinterest: Urban Outfitters, Mulberry, Topshop

Instagram: the good, the bad and the ugly

My first post on Instagram was a picture of my face, smiling awkwardly, filtered with hundreds of colours and completed with a thick black border. I had no idea what Instagram was. I'd found it via an article I'd read online about the creator of this new, cool image-sharing app, and I was intrigued enough to download it and try it for myself. That first photograph was me testing the capabilities of the application, figuring out whether it was something I would actually continue to use and how exactly it was going to create some form of addiction in my day. I used Instagram every few days to share the odd photograph of my life. My family pet, a vase of flowers, a countryside view from the car window. Those well-loved photos we are all taught to capture by our parents. But Instagram was a phenomenon, spreading like wildfire through everyone's mobile phones.

Instagram now has over 1 billion monthly users, each one sharing, learning, viewing and aspiring. And for some of those users, Instagram has become the basis of their career.

When the world was downloading and logging into Instagram
for the first time, it was looking for someone interesting to
follow. If it wasn't their favourite celebrity, it was the average
Joe who just happened to have an enticing profile. And thus,
a number of Instagram profiles experienced enormous growth
for a number of years, while the platform grew and changed.
With fashion brands casting an eye over the good-looking
girl with half a million people watching her every move, it was
inevitable that some of these profiles would lead to full-time
career opportunities. They could charge thousands of pounds

to feature products, be invited on the coolest international trips and live a lifestyle they could never have dreamed of before.

For fashion and beauty brands, it opened up an entirely unexpected method of advertising: sponsoring the ordinary woman or man to feature products naturally and realistically to the followers they had gathered, who were interested in how they dressed and what they applied on their face. It was taking the generic model ambassador and making them completely accessible to the average person. They didn't have to look like a supermodel to get a flawless make-up base or to wear the latest clothing. Thus, Instagram marketing became big bucks overnight. Brands could directly target a particular audience with their message while building sales, brand awareness and a ton of brand excitement, loyalty and affiliation. It was a winning formula, for both the brand and the Instagram personality.

At this point, having over 800,000 people following my Instagram account still feels unfathomable. It's near enough the same number of people who live in Fiji. But with that number of followers comes a certain responsibility. While most users don't set out to become the next huge Instagram account, they can be catapulted to Instagram royalty often without warning. So there are Instagram users whose accounts are managed solely by themselves, without any particular concern for the people who may be watching.

It's been talked about repeatedly over the last few years: whether the picture-perfect lifestyles created on Instagram are painting an unrealistic image for younger people to follow. Slim, athletic models sunning themselves in Bora Bora in provocative poses, ladies with no stretch marks on their behinds and beauty gurus with no pores in sight. And while the industry knows that

Be social

Be social

Facetune and Photoshop mobile apps exist and can blur out any imperfections the Instagrammer needs to remove, there are still younger people who are comparing their real-life image to a photoshopped model. Stories emerge frequently of younger people starving themselves to achieve the bodies of their favourite Instagrammers. Yet many would argue that the majority of fitness Instagram accounts are promoting a healthy body image and lifestyle and providing some #fitspo. Take a second to think about how Instagram imagery makes you feel – happy, inspired, motivated? Or sad, jealous, envious, disgusted?

Everyone will have their own perception of the Instagram bubble, whether it has a positive or negative influence on users and how particular users should portray themselves online. I believe that as long as a person is being true to themselves and the style of imagery that their audience knows them for, then their account is theirs to do with as they wish. Some users create whimsical imagery or purposefully photoshopped images that resemble artwork. Not every photo is real life, and it doesn't have to be. I think it's the audience's understanding of the user's style, and what they can expect from them, that will lead to a more positive outcome. There is a certain responsibility to uphold for the sake of your users, but there should also be a responsibility on the side of the followers to choose the accounts they follow wisely. Ultimately the decision has to be yours, but here are a few of my tips for Instagram:

Be social

Instagram

. . . tips for happiness

1. If a particular account doesn't make you feel happy any more, unfollow them – regardless of whether they're your friend or someone you feel will take it personally. If their images are in some way affecting your mental health, it's better to unfollow.

2. Find people to follow who really do promote a sense of empowerment, inspiration, happiness, positivity – or whatever else you like to follow. You may love make-up gurus, but follow those you feel you can relate to or who inspire you to try new things, not the people who make you feel bad about yourself in some way. Be kind to yourself.

3. Post what you want (within reason) and when you want. If you don't want to play to the supposed tips or 'rules' for beating the Instagram algorithm, and you just want to enjoy it, then do so. You don't have to pretend to be someone you're not if it's not making you happy. If you don't want to edit your images or post a certain type of photo of yourself, then don't. You do you.

... tips for editing

1. You don't have to edit your photos at all if you do not want to. But I find that the majority of accounts with bigger followings will edit their pictures to a certain extent.

2. Use an app across all of your photos, so you can create a similar editing style. I prefer Lightroom for getting my colours right, Facetune for any spot correction, whitening or detail work I may want to do, and I also like to tweak my images in Instagram before I post them. But Photoshop Express and VSCO are also fantastic editing apps that I've used for years. The majority of editing I do now is in Lightroom on my laptop before I transfer the images over to my phone to post, but it's personal preference.

3. Make your photos unique and personal to you. Whether you add grain or a border, use a certain colour scheme, light flares down the side of your images or anything else you can think of that takes your fancy, make your images recognisable and distinctive.

. . . tips for growth

1. Creating a theme to your images will definitely help you to grow. You want new users to come along to your profile, see a beautiful set of curated images they can relate to or enjoy, and to hit the follow button before they leave. I find that a colour or subject theme helps massively with this.

2. Be consistent with your posting. If you only post every few days, no one new is going to be able to find or see your photos. The more consistently you post, and the more often you post, the more likely it is that new users will spot your photos.

3. Don't edit your captions after you have posted them. It seems to halt your visibility in the feeds.

4. Take photos on a phone or camera – there is no difference in how the app responds to them. However, users tend to prefer images taken 'in the moment', candidly and realistically, so using low depth of field to blur out your backgrounds isn't always loved as much as a more 'unprofessional' image on an iPhone.

5. Find the best times for your audience to see your photos and stick to a posting routine. It lets them know when you might post and it will help your visibility if your audience is active and engaging.

6. Use hashtags in the caption that are relevant to that photo. Using spam or irrelevant hashtags – like 'Instagood', for instance – will likely get your photo ranked lower by Instagram for looking spam-like. You can use up to 30 hashtags, but I'd recommend using the best 10. A mixture of keywords relating to your location, brands you're wearing, the mood or things you can see in the shot, e.g. #Eiffeltower, #Maldives, #Paris, #Macaron.

7. Tag the brands you are wearing in the photo. If they love your image, they may regram you. This was one of the ways I grew so quickly when I first joined Instagram.

8. Keep up with your stories and post frequently. I find the more I post on stories, the better my image engagement, so give it a try.

9. Instagram is about engagement, not just for you but for everyone else. If you're not engaging with anyone else, then you're probably going to lose out. Like, comment and chat with other Instagrammers. You never know, someone might see your comment and follow you because of it. The person whose photo you've commented on might follow you, too. And for Instagram, it shows them you're a real person who's frequently engaging with different people, and with quality comments, so it's going to help you out. I say 'quality comments' because, let's be honest, a heart emoji or 'Nice' doesn't have much gravitas.

Olivier Rousteing

April 2011

The creative directors conquer Instagram

In this modern age when personality, profiles and images are king, it is no surprise that fashion brands have also developed their own public faces. But often these faces aren't the paid models, promoting and attracting an audience to visit the store. Rather, they are the people behind the designs, the clothing and the creativity. It's time for the creative directors to shine; after all, true loyalty comes from developing authenticity and a closer relationship with the audience. Arguably, one of the reasons why Dior, Saint Laurent and Chanel especially have created such dedicated, admiring followers to this day is due to their famous creative directors: Christian Dior, Yves Henri Donat Mathieu-Saint-Laurent, Karl Lagerfeld and Gabrielle Chanel herself. If you give an audience a face to remember, they're bound to feel more connected.

And what better way to connect than via Instagram. Olivier Rousteing, appointed creative director of Balmain in 2011, has gathered 5 million Instagram followers and befriended the likes of Kim Kardashian and Kanye West. To give some perspective, the brand account alone has only a third more followers. Stefano Gabbana, one half of Dolce & Gabbana, posts to over 1 million followers and has become an icon of the brand due to his own social presence and highly active profile, although the Dolce & Gabbana account does reach over 16 million followers. Yet popular modern-wear brand Off White also has a creative director, Virgil Abloh, with a following boasting over half that of the brand.

The huge followings don't just stop at Instagram. Karl Lagerfeld, creative director of Chanel and Fendi as well as his own eponymous brand, hosts a Twitter following of 1.48 million, alongside Chanel's 13.2 million. Powerhouse businesswoman and fashion designer Victoria Beckham hosts an Instagram following of 18 million people alongside 3.1 million on Facebook.

It's clear that the personal lives of the creative directors behind our favourite brands are becoming more important to us than ever before. In previous years, to the ordinary consumer buying a new garment in a luxury store, it was the design or style of the garment that would determine whether they took it home with them or not. To the majority, it was not necessarily about who had designed the garment, but about the garment itself. Now, with the industry so competitive, the designers are becoming almost as famous as the brand, and it's a trend that is likely to continue. And if that means engagement in their brand is at an all-time high, why not? It certainly can't hurt to have a platform of millions to promote your latest collections.

Gabrielle Bonheur Chanel

The fashion journey of creative directors

Until I studied fashion, I had no idea that designers moved from brand to brand, especially when that designer has their own named brand to look after. I would never have realised that Alexander Wang also designed for Balenciaga, or that Yves Saint Laurent was the creative director for Dior in 1957. But it makes sense to keep ideas fresh and to reinvigorate continuous collections. Now that I know, I find it fascinating to follow the footprints of the biggest creative directors to see where they've been and where they are now. So I've compiled this list for others interested in following the designers behind their favourite brands. Bear in mind that when creative directors are listed as serving to the 'present', it refers to 2018, and positions may well have changed since this book's publication. It's not a conclusive list of every luxury house or every possible director – that would be a book in itself. Instead, it's a list of brands that I feel have a really interesting history of directors, and often show a progression of designers moving from one to another within the list.

Brands and their directors

Alexander Wang: Alexander Wang, 2007–present.

Anthony Vaccarello: Anthony Vaccarello, 2008–present.

Balenciaga: Cristóbal Balenciaga, 1919–1968. Closed until 1986. Michel Goma, 1987–1992. Josephus Thimister, 1992–1997. Nicolas Ghesquière, 1997–2012. Alexander Wang, 2012–2015. Demna Gvasalia, 2015–present.

Balmain: Pierre Balmain, 1945–1982. Erik Mortensen, 1982–1990. Hervé Pierre Braillard, 1990–1992. Oscar de la Renta, 1993–2002. Christophe Lebourg, 2003–2006. Christophe Decarnin, 2006–2011. Olivier Rousteing, 2011–present.

Burberry: Thomas Burberry, 1856–1917. Christopher Bailey, 2001–2018. Riccardo Tisci, 2018–present.

Calvin Klein: Calvin Klein, 1968–2003. Francisco Costa, 2003–2016. Raf Simons, 2016–present.

Céline: Céline Viviana, 1945–1997. Michael Kors, 1997–2005.

Roberto Menichetti, 2005–2006. Ivana Omazic, 2006–2008. Phoebe Philo, 2008–2018. Hedi Slimane, 2018–present.

Chanel: Gabrielle Bonheur ´Coco´ Chanel, 1909–1971. Various designers, 1971–1983. Karl Lagerfeld, 1983–present.

Chloé: Gaby Aghion, 1952–1985. Martine Sitbon, 1987–1992. Karl Lagerfeld, 1992–1997. Stella McCartney, 1997–2001. Phoebe Philo, 2001–2006. Paulo Melim Andersson, 2006–2008. Hannah MacGibbon, 2008–2011. Clare Waight Keller, 2011–2017. Natacha Ramsay-Levi, 2017–present.

Dior: Christian Dior, 1946–1957. Yves Saint Laurent, 1957–1960. Marc Bohan, 1960–1989. Gianfranco Ferré, 1989–1997. John Galliano, 1997–2011. Bill Gaytten, 2011–2012. Raf Simons, 2012–2015. Maria Grazia Chiuri, 2016–present.

Dior Homme: Marc Bohan, 1970–1992. Patrick Lavoix, 1992–2000. Hedi Slimane, 2000–2007. Kris Van Assche, 2007–2018. Kim Jones, 2018–present.

Fendi: Karl Lagerfeld, 1977–present.

Be social

Alexander Wang

Maria Grazia Chiuri

Givenchy: Hubert de Givenchy, 1952–1995. John Galliano, 1995–1996. Alexander McQueen, 1996–2001. Julien MacDonald, 2001–2004. Riccardo Tisci, 2005–2017. Clare Waight Keller, 2017–present.

Gucci: Guccio Gucci, 1921–1953. Aldo and Rodolfo Gucci, 1953–1983. Maurizio Gucci, 1983–1989. Dawn Mello, 1989–1994. Tom Ford, 1994–2004. Frida Giannini, 2005–2014. Alessandro Michele, 2015–present.

John Galliano: John Galliano, 1988–2011.

J. W. Anderson: Jonathan Anderson, 2008–present.

Karl Lagerfeld: Karl Lagerfeld, 1974–present.

Lanvin: Jeanne Lanvin, 1889–1946. Antonio Canovas del Castillo, 1950–1963. Jules François Crahay, 1964–1984. Maryll Lanvin, 1981–1989. Claude Montana, 1990–1992. Dominique Morlotti, 1992–2001. Alber Elbaz, 2001–2015. Bouchra Jarrar, 2016–2017. Olivier Lapidus, 2017–present.

Loewe: Jonathan Anderson, 2013–present.

Louis Vuitton: Louis Vuitton, 1854–1892. Georges Vuitton, 1892–1936. Gaston-Louis Vuitton, 1936–1997. Marc Jacobs, 1997–2013. Nicolas Ghesquière, 2013–present.

Maison Martin Margiela: Martin Margiela, 1988–2014. John Galliano, 2014–present.

Marc Jacobs: Marc Jacobs, 1986–present.

Moschino: Franco Moschino, 1983–1994. Rossella Jardini, 1994–2013. Jeremy Scott, 2013–present.

Oscar de la Renta: Óscar Arístides Renta Fiallo, 1965–2014. Peter Copping, 2014–2016. Laura Kim and Fernando Garcia, 2016–present.

Stella McCartney: Stella McCartney, 2001–present.

Stella McCartney

Tom Ford: Tom Ford, 2004–present.

Valentino: Valentino Garavani, 1960–2007. Maria Grazia Chiuri, 2008–2016. Pierpaolo Piccioli, 2008–present.

Versace: Gianni Versace, 1972–1997. Donatella Versace, 1997–present.

Versus Versace: Donatella Versace, 1989–2005. Christopher Kane, 2009–2012. Jonathan Anderson, 2013–2014. Anthony Vaccarello, 2014–2016. Donatella Versace, 2016–present.

Vetements: Demna Gvasalia, 2009–present.

Yves Saint Laurent: Yves Saint Laurent, 1961–1998. Alber Elbaz, 1998–1999. Tom Ford, 1999–2004. Stefano Pilati, 2004–2012. Hedi Slimane, 2012–2016. Anthony Vaccarello, 2016–present.

The clothing-haul obsession

The first YouTube haul I filmed was in May 2013, after eight months of blogging and a crazy excitement to show everyone what I had been out to buy that day. And it was the haul-video concept that initially got me hooked on YouTube. The girl or guy next door in their bedroom, chatting about their latest sale buys or the abundance of clothing they picked up yesterday in Primark. The haul video started out a lot more modest and high street. Boohoo, Missguided, Primark and ASOS hauls were the videos you would see creep into your subscription box most days. It was a way to see what your favourite YouTube friend had bought on their shopping trip and what you, too, could buy if you wanted to dress like they did. I was obsessed. Especially when it came to beauty. I remember buying hundreds of pounds´ worth of make-up back in the early days of my

Amelia Liana

Suzie Bonaldi

TOPSHOP
HAUL

obsession — often purchasing a whole face of make-up that I'd seen on my favourite beauty guru so I could get their look. It's addictive!

There are so many people making YouTube videos now that it's become a fashion marketer's dream. Three hundred hours of content are uploaded onto YouTube every minute — and I can only imagine how many of those videos include someone wearing particular garments or accessories. Whether you're watching a specific YouTube haul, or even a daily vlog of your most-loved creator, they're bound to be wearing or using something that might take your fancy. And if they're helpful to their audience, they will have linked that item in the description box 'down below'. Purchase, done. It's not like seeing a static image of the garment on an online mannequin, or even on the body of a model walking up and down a catwalk — you are seeing the garment on a person you are inspired by, how it moves, how it flatters, how it fits and if it might suit you.

The largest YouTube channel in the world has over 60 million followers, with a focus on gaming and comedy. That's how massive YouTube has become. The largest UK female YouTube channel, Zoella, surpassed the 12 million mark in 2018 and appeals to fashion, beauty and lifestyle lovers. While Instagram offers visual inspiration, at the moment it doesn't have a seamless click-through ability to buy the items shown within the images – a feature that YouTubers like Zoella are able to capitalise on, linking their outfits for their audience of millions to devour. Four in ten people are said to visit the store mentioned in a YouTube haul, so if a brand can get their dress in the hands of a YouTuber with some pretty huge influence, they are singing.

My own haul videos are still some of my most popular. It's like being a personal shopper for your audience, trawling through pages of new-in collections to find the hidden gems. It's a winning formula and one I think audiences will continue to love. My personal style has dramatically changed over the years, definitely in part due to my interest in clothing hauls. They showed me how to style items and what accessories were the best of the season, and elevated my confidence to dress how I wanted. Don't worry, marketers, the haul is going nowhere.

Be social

How and why to start your own YouTube channel

Have a reason to film

If you feel you have something to give to an audience – a skill, information on a particular topic, life advice – or maybe you live a life you feel others would find fun to watch, then why not? You will spend a lot of time speaking straight into a camera, on your own in a quiet room. It's odd, but you need to remember that there will be someone out there who will watch it, so really, you're speaking to them.

Be yourself

When I first started my channel, I found it so difficult to be natural. My best friend told me she couldn't watch my videos because they made her cringe – she wasn't being a bitch; it was because she knew I wasn't being myself and it was hard for her to watch a completely different me. We've laughed about this a lot over the years. Six months later, I had settled in, found my natural voice and it was just like watching the real me, so when she told me she could now watch and enjoy my videos, I knew I'd reached a point where I was being myself. Every YouTuber needs to get to that stage.

Be organised

Uploading regularly, at a set time or with a set number of videos per week, gives your audience something to come back for. If you only upload once in a blue moon, your audience doesn't know what to expect or when to find your uploads, especially those who are busy and don't have time to check up on YouTube every hour of the day. Equally, keep your channel looking organised and clear – use simple playlist titles to group particular types of videos. For instance, I have Fashion Hauls, Make-up Tutorials, Lookbooks, Vlogs, etc. And have a banner and picture on your profile that makes it look legit, but also attractive to a new audience.

Be responsible

Make sure that what you upload isn't going to upset, offend or hurt anyone. We all heard the news about a particular YouTuber uploading videos about suicide victims, harassing Japanese tourists and generally being completely disrespectful. Don't be that guy. Show your intelligence or show your humour or just show the real you, but don't use your channel to bring others down. That's not a career with longevity, and never will be.

Where to binge on clothing hauls

If you're new to YouTube and looking for fashion creators to follow, then of course I'm going to shamelessly plug myself — just search YouTube for Inthefrow. But there are many other girls and guys around the world making awesome fashion hauls, so it's hard to nail down just a few that I love. If you fancy a binge, just type 'fashion haul' or 'luxury fashion haul' into the YouTube search bar. For more specific recommendations, here are a few ladies I would absolutely recommend you check out:

Amelia Liana

A good friend of mine and a gal with a gorgeous fashion sense, beautiful luxury additions to her closet and just the warmest heart. She picks the most stunning holiday pieces, summer outfits and high-street to luxury items you wish you'd found first.

Ashley Brooke

A fabulous US YouTuber whose style I feel is similar to my own. I love her hair, the way she chats about the clothing and the way she shoots her videos so that you can see every outfit as she wears it. She mixes every brand out there with a little bit of luxury accessorising and just owns every ensemble.

Chriselle Lim

I have to mention Chriselle, as her style is flawless and I adore bingeing on any of her videos. And with her own studio and team to help film and edit, she makes the most fantastic, polished fashion content that you won't be able to get enough of.

Fashion Mumblr

Josie is feminine, elegant and that girl next door with a beautiful fashion collection. If you love to look put-together and refined on the daily, Josie definitely has a style you'll adore.

HelloOctober

Suzie's hauls are to the point, filled with beautiful, lust-worthy clothing and accessories and a lot of upper-high-street to high-street brands that most will love. Plus, she's super-sassy and a cool gal to watch.

Jenn Im

Jenn is a Korean-American YouTuber who has long been a favourite of mine. Her unique editing style and calming voice just make me want to be a lot cooler so I can pull off her style. She mixes thrift items with gorgeous new ones, clothing from her own line Eggie and high-street to luxury clothing styles.

Be social

Samantha Maria

Chriselle Lim

Be social

Megan Ellaby

Megan Ellaby

Megan is a fellow Manchester gal and someone who always puts a smile on my face. Her style is quirky, fun and alternative, mixing vintage finds with the more unusual pieces that you may initially bypass, but when you see her style them, you'll be like, dayum, that looks amazing! No one does Eighties or retro styling like Megan.

Patricia Bright

Patricia makes some of the funniest hauls you will see on YouTube. She tries on and critiques the clothes as she goes, and her sassy, no-bull attitude makes her videos laugh-out-loud hilarious.

Samantha Maria

Sammi was the first gal I followed on YouTube – and I've told her this umpteen times. She was one of my biggest inspirations and, luckily, I can now call her a friend. Her fashion hauls and try-on videos are some of my absolute favourites. Her style is girly but cool, casual and then sometimes more elegant. She's got the whole package.

Patricia Bright

157

Jennifer Lawrence (centre) with the cast and director of *Red Sparrow*

The fashion news goes viral

It was Saturday morning, and the headlines hit the social feeds regarding the allegations against Mario Testino and Bruce Weber. Two of the fashion world's favourite photographers, both with long-standing relationships with Condé Nast, were both under fire for alleged claims of sexual misconduct, and the story went viral. While both denied the claims when the news stories landed, *Vogue* US, and more specifically Anna Wintour herself, swiftly issued an official statement online saying that *Vogue* would be suspending their working relationships with both photographers for the foreseeable future. Those who claimed to be affected had spoken out online. As soon as it's online, it's online forever, and the consequences are unforgiving.

A week or two later, in February 2018, Jennifer Lawrence was in the spotlight, for wearing a stunning Versace dress to a London photocall. While the four male co-starring actors and director of *Red Sparrow* stood around her in jackets, she was cold-shouldered and jacket-less on a freezing, snowy London rooftop. Twitter and Facebook were in uproar. The viral world spoke: 'This picture of Jennifer Lawrence sums up what it's like to be a woman in Hollywood', 'Please give Jennifer Lawrence a dang coat'. According to some Twitter users, how dare these men don warm jackets while Jennifer was left to freeze? Jennifer raged on Facebook to express her exasperation at the 'ridiculous' comments, writing, 'That Versace dress was fabulous, you think I'm going to cover that gorgeous dress up with a coat and a scarf? I was outside for 5 minutes. I would have stood in the snow for that dress because I love fashion and that was my choice.' It was good promo for the dress, at least. Personally, I've stood outside numerous times, freezing to the bone in a beautiful dress, to get the perfect picture. Maybe I'm crazy, or maybe Jennifer has a very good point.

Whether a news story breaks on *Vogue*, a blog post article gets picked up by the *Daily Mail* or someone posts a tweet that a person of influence can retweet and forward on, that story is going to be seen by huge numbers of people, faster than you can say 'delete'. That is how fashion news is shared, found and searched for now. I always scan the latest news bulletins on Twitter before looking at any other news source online. It's reactive, up to the minute and, in some cases, entirely live. You can keep up with the story directly as the information is flooding in.

We're also at a place now where everything anyone writes online needs to be thoroughly checked and checked again. It means the end of real spontaneity, but a badly worded tweet can end someone's career or spark outrage and offence within a multitude of communities. Huge changes will also need to happen in the fashion industry in relation to the responsibilities and behaviours of those in power. Which I'm hoping will lead to a safer space for all.

Fashion stories that went viral

O   The news of Edward Enninful's new position at UK *Vogue* in 2017 was shared and celebrated online by everyone from models to editors to celebrities. It marked a big change in *Vogue*'s future and creative vision, and so many influential voices were excited for a shake-up.

Edward Enninful

○ Donatella Versace brought back the original Nineties' supermodels to close the Versace S/S18 show in Milan. Naomi, Claudia, Cindy, Carla and Helena were all dressed in gold Versace gowns and walked the length of the runway with Donatella to celebrate the 20th anniversary of Gianni Versace's death. The number of Instastories, live feeds, images and news stories were in the masses, making it the most viral moment of fashion month for years.

○ A small group of *Vogue* US editors decided to drag down the blogging industry mid-Milan Fashion Week 2016, harshly branding bloggers as the reason for a future death of style. See the section on 'Susie bursts the fashion bubble' on page 256 to read all about that juicy news.

Be social

Versace S/S18

○ Dolce & Gabbana brought 'the Millennials' – aka YouTubers, Instagrammers, socialites, bloggers and influencers – onto their catwalk in 2017, dressed in ready-to-wear outfits. It was one of the first times that the two worlds had collided, and the luxury fashion space was acknowledging the influence of such young people. The news was everywhere online, as soon as the first Millennial's beautifully polished and embellished heel hit the Dolce & Gabbana runway.

Be culturally aware & diverse

Now is the time to use your style, and your voice, to make a statement about the issues that are important to you. The Internet has become a soapbox; somewhere for people to congregate, share, learn and discuss their opinions. And thus, many issues that have long gone ignored in the fashion industry are being shouted about from the rooftops, leaving the blissfully ignorant nowhere to hide. Stories of inclusivity, diversity and awareness are finally reaching centre stage in an industry that has long needed a push towards progression. Time is up on the hypocrisy, ignorance and narrow-mindedness of previous decades. It's up to us to use our voices to share the message and continue the change.

Be culturally aware and diverse

Iskra Lawrence

Admiring all shapes and sizes

When I was in my teens my mum was a curvier size 16–18, and we would venture to the Trafford Centre together to buy ourselves a few treats. I can vividly remember her frustration and upset, as she had only a handful of stores she could visit that catered for larger sizes for mature women. And back then they weren't always the most fashion-forward. Wallis, M&S, Next and Debenhams were in that handful, but otherwise the high street was lacking in clothing stores that specifically catered to the plus-sized market. In fact, the term plus-sized wasn't even a thing.

As the online world grew, it brought a rise in plus-sized-specific retailers. Simply Be, in 1999, was one of the first retailers to design clothing for women between sizes 12 and 32, capitalising on an unexplored marketplace. It was a wise move,

Be culturally aware and diverse

seeing as 58 per cent of the UK female market in 2015 was said to fall into the plus-size categories and the average UK female is a size 16, according to PWC. Many retailers have followed suit, with Forever 21, Gap, Banana Republic and Nike, to name a few, extending their clothing sizes, and ASOS stocking 20 plus-sized brands alongside their own collection, ASOS Curve. It's an amazing investment, considering that in 2017 the UK plus-size market was worth £6.6 billion.

Australian retailer Aerie has completely embraced beauty in all shapes and sizes, launching a campaign in 2014 with the tagline: 'The girl in this photo has not been retouched. The real you is sexy.' Their campaign imagery promoted beautiful women with cellulite, dimples, stretch marks and imperfections, just like all of us.

But it's the rise in plus-sized models being cast for huge brand campaigns that is creating the most excitement. We are all aware that previously there has been a focus on tall, slender models for the majority of mass-media advertisements. According to various model casting agencies, since early 2017 they have been getting continuous calls for their plus-sized models – probably because of the success of the Aerie campaign, the 20-per-cent-plus sales increase they gained and pressure from the social audience. Since that campaign, plus-size casting in beauty and fashion campaigns has increased, a number of brands have decided to reduce retouching and the likes of Target have cast a full range of models to reflect the diversity of their customers.

Everyone is beautiful, regardless of their size or imperfections, and it's a message we need to be sharing more. It's empowering for the percentage of women all over the world who fall into plus-sized clothing categories to finally have role models in their favourite magazines, wearing the dresses of some of the biggest luxury designers.

The values of the customer have changed. They demand to feel included, accepted and adored, and social media has allowed them a place to vent and, most importantly, to publicly shame. The bare minimum is no longer acceptable. Brands are having to make changes in the sizes they offer and who represents them in their adverts, and in the majority of cases, it's working in their favour. The plus-sized audience need to be able to relate to the models and see themselves wearing the clothing they're displaying. Up until recently, almost 50 per cent of the population was being left out of the fashion circles, and while there's still a long way to go, this route to a more diversified fashion landscape is a truly exciting one.

Where to shop for stylish plus-sized fashion

Aside from the brands mentioned on page 168, here are a number of other brands that are producing fashion-forward and beautiful clothes for the plus-sized market:

Anna Scholz

Designer of fashion pieces with unique prints and timeless styles for the plus-sized woman.

City Chic at Evans

Australian fashion house City Chic has moved its stores to the US as well as selling exclusively via Evans stores in the UK. Evans is also a specialist in the UK plus-size retail space.

Coast for Simply Be

An exclusive line of plus-sized Coast fashion for Simply Be.

Good American

Khloé Kardashian's denim line for ladies between size 0 and 24.

Michael Kors

Stocked in Macys, Michael Kors launched a specific plus-sized collection for the curvier lady.

Navabi

A department store for a number of fashionable designer plus-sized brands.

New Look Curves

An extended line of the current New Look styles, perfect for the lady who loves the regular New Look collections.

Studio Eight

The sister brand and plus-size offering of Phase Eight.

Justin Timberlake and Jessica Biel

#TimesUp

Every actor and actress, director, producer and guest pulls up
to the 2018 Baftas red carpet in their chauffeured car dressed
specifically and purposefully in black. It's a sign of solidarity,
everyone standing together to make a bold statement. 'Time's
Up' – the movie industry will no longer brush the dark secrets
of its famous faces under the carpet. Anyone who has had
their sordid history purposefully ignored will soon be outed and
the practices that were long able to hide in the shadows will
be brought into the light. The hashtag is bold and threatening,
and purposefully so. It marks a moment of empowerment and
strength, and has opened up a conversation that has long
gone unspoken. The hashtag and cause that lit the flame,
#metoo, gathered so much traction from the online world, with
anyone and everyone sharing their own upsetting accounts

Prabal Gurung A/W17

of sexual assault and harassment. And due to the few brave voices coming from the film industry, a huge change was able to happen. People found their voices, shared their stories and made it impossible for the culprits to hide.

All the attendees of the Baftas 2018 stood together that day as a message and sign of their allegiance to the cause. Similarly, at the Grammys 2018 a host of attending celebrities again sported black attire and white roses to show their solidarity with #TimesUp.

But the hashtags mean so much more than just that. The 'Me Too' movement is a conversation, a voice for everyone who has had to endure an experience of sexual harassment or violence of any kind. 'Time's Up' was founded to fight for the cause of workplace equality, sexual harassment and equal opportunities for women and people of colour. It aims straight for the root of the issue, working to resolve power imbalances that may lead to harassment behaviour in the first place.

This is not the first time that fashion has played a part in an important movement. In fact, while fashion enables us to look unique and different to our neighbour, it can also help us be seen as part of a community. Just think of how symbolic the rainbow flag has become of the people it represents, the varying colours symbolising the diversity in the community and the pride in their individuality. Flags were initially designed as an identification mark or a patriotic symbol, and it is incredible that the enormously diverse LGBTQ+ community now has their own mark of solidarity, ownership and identity.

Likewise, a number of charities, such as Fashion Targets Breast Cancer, have designed T-shirts and jumpers emblazoned with slogans that have become symbols of their online charity campaigns, encouraging others to take part, wear the T-shirt, take a picture and share it around the web, and therefore show solidarity while sharing an important message. And for Fashion Week A/W17, Prabal Gurung sent his models down the runway wearing statement T-shirts reading 'The future is female' and 'I am an immigrant', inspired by the New York Women's March. These are empowering statements that are being shared and supported profusely all over the world.

So while fashion certainly has the power to divide, it is better used as a way to bring us all together.

A cry for inclusivity and diversity

The voices lower and the lights come up; it's time for the Prada show to start. It's February 2018 and taking to the catwalk is Anok Yai, the first black model to open a Prada show since Naomi Campbell in 1997. It's a sign that the fashion industry is finally moving forwards regarding increased diversity and inclusivity. An industry that was once primarily caucasian, led by caucasian designers, is slowly becoming a platform to display the beauty in variety.

And luckily it doesn't end with the fashion industry. The beauty industry has also taken enormous steps over the last few years to deliver more diverse collections for their loyal fans. It's the reason why Fenty Beauty was so adored on its release, uniquely launching 40 foundation shades that suited a wide range of skin tones, from the palest porcelain to the deepest ebony. People want diversity, they want others to feel included and they will no longer stand for excuses. L'Oréal Paris was one of the first brands to champion diversity, casting spokesmodels with varying backgrounds, ethnicities, genders and religions, and with their True Match foundation campaign they showed that every skin tone was beautiful, different and catered for within their product range. If a brand isn't catering for everyone, then in the tight online beauty communities, the backlash often reaches viral proportions. I have discussed this with various beauty PR teams and I've been delighted when they've spoken of their upcoming foundation releases in an abundance of shades and a real focus on true inclusivity. It certainly looks like the change is accelerating.

Anok Yai for Prada A/W18

Adwoa Aboah

Edward Enninful, with his famous move to *Vogue* UK in 2017, swiftly made it clear that big changes needed to happen. With his first cover confidently displaying the most famous model of the moment, Adwoa Aboah, and the employment of a fresh team and contributing writers including Naomi Campbell, he published the new *Vogue* with a bang. The majority of the industry rejoiced and *Vogue* was brought full throttle into the now.

It is momentous to see these changes happening, with consumers and brands together finally standing up for the rights of everyone. Whereas before, the thoughts of the masses were not heard and their cries for change had no outlet for broadcast, social media and online broadcasting has offered an influential platform from which to shout. And people are shouting louder than ever. The fashion industry can no longer brush away the small voices querying their diversity; these cries now come with hundreds of thousands of retweets, likes and tabloid coverage. It is a whole new level of feedback and opinions. People are just as angry and frustrated as they have always been; they're just finally having their voices heard. And those designers or brands who are not listening will be vilified and left behind. The time is now to build a platform for change.

Six moments when the fashion industry stepped closer to inclusivity

1. Gap launched their Bridging the Gap campaign in 2017, directed and styled by *Vogue*'s Edward Enninful and featuring nine out of ten models of colour. A huge step forward for the industry and a beautiful campaign to boot.

2. Helmut Lang cast a widely diverse group of models and industry stars for their 2017 campaign, Seen By: The Artist Series, including 60 per cent non-white models, three transgender creatives and two females over 50, to convey a new message for the brand.

3. For their #DGPalermo campaign in 2017, 63 per cent of the Dolce & Gabbana models were racially diverse, with one plus-sized model included in the line-up. This followed their equally inclusive Fall 17 catwalk show.

Be culturally aware and diverse

Gap's 'Bridging the Gap' campaign, 2017

Chromat S/S17

4.   For Spring 2017, five plus-sized models walked the runway for Christian Soriano and Chromat, including a model wearing anti-chafing bands around her thighs, also included in gift bags for all guests.

5.   In May 2018 *Vogue* launched a cover of nine diverse models of varying races, backgrounds, religions and sizes. To Edward Enninful, it represented the idea that anything is possible.

6.   River Island launched the #LabelsAreForClothes campaign in 2018, dismissing stereotypes and casting a diverse roster of younger and older, petite and curvier, male, female and gender-neutral models to highlight that no one individual needs to be labelled.

Ban the fur

'Fur? I'm out of that . . . I don't want to kill animals to make fashion. It doesn't feel right.'
Donatella Versace, 2018

And the fashion world took an inward sigh of relief. Since Gucci, Tom Ford, Givenchy and Michael Kors all made anti-fur statements in 2018, the cruelty-free consumers have been hoping that the most glamorous fashion houses would follow suit. This statement from Donatella in an interview for the *Economist* marks another sign of change: that even the most lavish of brands doesn't need to use fur — and neither should anyone else.

Versace A/W17

Fake fur at Gucci S/S18

For London Fashion Week S/S18, 86 per cent of brands didn't feature fur. I wish this number was closer to 100 per cent, but the list of huge fashion houses that have strict no-fur policies is steadily rising and the majority of high-street stores also adhere to this principle, including luxury department stores such as Selfridges, Liberty and Net-A-Porter.

So the pressure is mounting on those designers who still feel that fur is relevant, necessary or excusable in the current age. It's a shift that has been accelerated by the pressures from the online world. There are louder, angrier and bigger numbers of frustrated voices than ever before, reaching the high towers of these fashion brands. The more the media and online audience voice their disgust at such brutal fur-usage policies, the fewer places these brands will have left to hide – apart from behind their mink skins. I'm optimistic that within five years we will see a fur-free fashion industry once and for all.

No-fur luxury fashion brands

Armani	Net-A-Porter
Calvin Klein	Ralph Lauren
Furla	Selfridges
Givenchy	Shrimps
Gucci	Stella McCartney
Hugo Boss	The Kooples
Kate Spade	Tom Ford
Lacoste	Tommy Hilfiger
Liberty	Versace
Michael Kors	Vivienne Westwood

RULE 5

Be innovative

No one ever created something unique by staying in their comfort zone. You need to get out of your bubble, see what's happening around you and down a big bottle of inspiration. The best ideas, concepts and outfits have come from a place of awareness and a desire to try something new, and when it comes to the fashion industry, innovation can be the key to success. Be experimental, try new styles, and don't be afraid to use the inspiration you've gained and run with it. Technologies are being adapted and enhanced for our benefit, so enjoy them. By embracing the latest innovations, you can reap the rewards of this exciting new digital space.

If you ignore the movement altogether, you're missing out on new and exciting experiences. Brands and designers need to stay ahead of the race; if they're happy to just go with the flow, they're bound to get left behind. It's time for everyone to be brave and lead the innovation. The chances are that people will follow in your footsteps.

NikeID and the new customisation

Picture this. It's 1999. It's eight years before the iPhone. MSN messenger has just been released and home computers are only now becoming more popular household items. You've probably got your first, oversized desktop computer sat on your desk and it's running frustratingly slowly. But you use every last ounce of your dial-up connection, and patience, for the opportunity to design your own customised pair of shoes on the NikeID site. You select the colours of the laces, the tongue, the insole and the heel and enter your card details into the website to purchase your one-of-a-kind pair of sneakers. This is probably one of the coolest things you have ever done.

The launch of NikeID was one of the earliest meetings between fashion and technology, when the Internet became an integrated part of a fashion brand's strategy. The majority

of consumers in 1999 were struggling to pay for online gig tickets and worrying about where their card details were being stored. But Nike pulled their consumer onto their online store to offer them a service unlike anything they had seen before. I remember stumbling upon the NikeID site at that time and it blew my mind. The colour-selection task of the fashion designer was placed in the consumer's hands and the shoes could be delivered to your house within three-to-five weeks. I was sold! Nike were unbelievably ahead of the curve.

NikeID was first to launch this new and exciting online customisation concept, later updating it to a user-friendly

flash site in 2005 and harnessing the power of their loyal fans
to offer them something completely unique. The first version of
the site was clunky and cumbersome, but it was an experience
unlike any other. It revolutionised the concept of product
customisation forever, and since then a multitude of brands
have taken inspiration from it.

I would have bought myself a pair of custom Nikes if I
was a trainer wearer and had a credit card to purchase with
at 10 years old. The first personalised item I bought was a
backpack that I wore throughout school. Nowhere near as cool,
but I was happy adding my Bon Jovi and Aerosmith patches
to my Quiksilver backpack as a sign of my allegiance to the
rock-music gods. It was the first time I made an item my own
and I totally got the hype. It's so fun to feel like you're wearing
something that you've made your mark on.

While lots of consumers love to feel a sense of belonging,
and in some cases to own the same piece of clothing that
somebody else has sported publicly, there are many others
who prefer individuality. The millennial generation is far more
liberal than their elders, less likely to follow a religion, specific
ideologies or a particular political party. They're interested
primarily in their own individual views and beliefs, and they
want to disaffiliate from the masses. The Internet has only

helped spur on this movement with the likes of personal profiles and outspoken social sharing.

This idea of individualism has seeped through into the everyday consumer's fashion and lifestyle choices, hence the rise in customisable apparel and personalised finishes. A handful of well-loved brands such as Levi's, Tommy Hilfiger and Coach have brought customisation stations into their stores to enable customers to patch, stud or cut their garment into something unique while they wait. And online, an assortment of retailers have become known as the one-stop shop for customisable items, from clothing to furniture. Not on the High Street and Etsy have both provided the ability to tailor products for the consumer who desires a one-of-a-kind piece. Anya Hindmarch further continued the trend, adding a 'Build a Bag' station to her global stockists, where customers can pick and choose straps, tassels, stickers and various colours to create their own personalised piece. From customisable Christmas baubles to wrapping paper printed with the giftee's name at Selfridges, and from colour to slogan, print or silhouette, it looks like we're ready to put our stamp on every possible surface.

But without Nike and their innovative move to online customisation, would the fashion world have spotted this huge trend as quickly? Nike started a revolution and it has only spiralled since then. It brought the consumer closer to the brand than they could ever have been before and rewarded them with something that no one else could buy. A special gift for years of loyalty. A customised pair of kicks.

The best places to go for personalised items

- Coach: Your most loved Coach bag from years ago, or the cute new trend piece you just bought – in the flagship stores, you can get your bag personalised and repaired.

- Levi's: Rips, tears, studs, distressing, patches; you name it, you get it.

- Louis Vuitton: I mean, who wouldn't want a LV printed tote with their initials embroidered slap bang in the centre?

- Monica Vinader Jewellery: Your lover's initials, your mum's name, your baby's birth date – whatever you want can be etched into the metal of your choice in the jewellery piece you love the most.

- Nixon: If you ever wanted to build your own watch, including your choice of face, casing, strap, bezel and custom engraving, then Nixon has two stores in London that could make you very happy indeed.

- Tods: If you're looking for a pair of shoes unlike anyone else's, you can customise your own Tods Gommino's from start to finish, from stitching to colours to initials.

The fashion catwalk in your bedroom

I spent many months looking at the innovative functions of fashion websites when I was writing my PhD. I was so interested in how certain features could persuade or encourage a shopper to become a consumer, and so I interviewed lots of people as to what they liked or didn't like online. Not surprisingly, the fashion catwalk was one of their favourite things, and it's mine too. Seeing a piece of clothing drape or react to movement, how it fits on a body shape, its length or silhouette and its true tone in the lighting – it's one of the main things that makes me hit 'Add to bag'. I'm more likely to buy from stores that offer this mini video of the item over those that don't. If they can't be bothered to show me what it looks like on a model, even just in pictures, then I can't be bothered to spend my money.

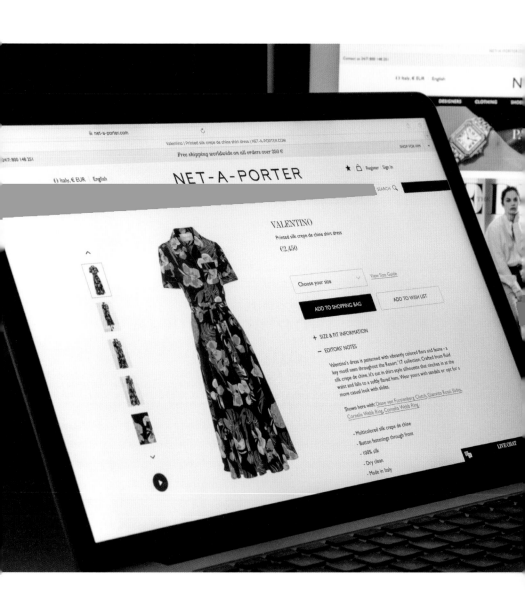

At this point, with the advancements in technology, it's not good enough for websites to only offer one image of a product. Side views, 360-degree views and especially worn views of the item on a model are paramount to the consumer's engagement and interest in a product. I didn't need to write a PhD to figure that one out! So it's surprising that many websites still only offer one image of a garment, a pair of shoes or a handbag. Retailers that don't offer a modelled view of sunglasses – now that just riles me up.

Of course, there are also the websites who are doing it the right way.

Net-A-Porter is way ahead of the game, adding a clean, non-modelled view of the item, close-ups of the material, modelled views of the item from various angles and the pièce de résistance, the 15-second video clip of the model moving in the item, styled with accessories and set against a white backdrop. It might take longer to film and edit, but it will also encourage the majority of shoppers to decide to buy it. It's worth it and I'm sold.

The more confidence and the less risk the customer feels when they're shopping, the more likely they are to purchase. So take away their worries about the fit, the colour being the wrong tone, the shape not being flattering and whether they could actually wear it and you're bound to have even more happy customers. We just want to be inspired and shown both the benefits and how it will fit into our lifestyle.

As a consumer, if you're buying something and you're not sure whether you'll love it or not, click to watch the catwalk video. If they don't have one, move on to a website that stocks that product and does care about your shopping experience. You're far less likely to send it back that way, so it will benefit not only you, but also the website in the long run.

Be innovative

The best shopping experiences

ASOS

The gamechanger. ASOS pioneered the interactive movement, offered free returns early in the game and tried to build an immersive space for their customers to hang out.

Away

For cute carry-ons that you've probably seen all over your Instagram feeds, this website is really brilliant for giving you all the info and angles you need.

Everlane

This site is so good. Close-ups, videos, alternative angles and what to wear it with. Super-handy.

Matches Fashion

A favourite of mine, and a luxury haven for products. But they have really understood what their customer wants when they're shopping, with all the angles, videos and style advice.

Missguided

An affordable female fave. They've got their modelled imagery spot on alongside a video, and a section to shop the whole look. There's nothing more annoying than seeing a pair of shoes on the model only to find they're not linked anywhere on the page, or the whole website for that matter.

Net-A-Porter

As I've mentioned, they spend a lot of time removing the risk for the consumer and I love them for it.

Warby Parker

That thing I mentioned about sunglasses sites that don't even show you what they look like on ... well, this site is the total opposite of that. It has nailed the experience for customers looking for frames. A model literally follows your mouse by moving her head, so you can see every angle of the glasses.

Be innovative

Sophia Amoruso

June 2008

Sophia Amoruso
launches Nasty Gal

If you've read *#GirlBoss*, or watched the Netflix show, you'll
already be clued up on this one. Throw back to 2006 when
a quirky and youthful Sophia Amoruso was working as a
campus safety host in San Francisco, when she spotted a
trend for vintage clothing among the eBay community. eBay
had launched in 1995 and was fast becoming a reselling
phenomenon. If you haven't bought or sold something on eBay
yourself, I'm pretty sure you'll know someone who has. Anything
from old cars to used computers are traded, and for vintage
clothing it was and still is a fashion collector's dream. Amoruso
didn't know it yet, but selling a vintage leather jacket on her
eBay store would lead her to create one of the most famous
online success stories — Nasty Gal.

Within a year of eBay selling, the young entrepreneur had built up a social following on Myspace of 60,000 followers, and by the next year she'd moved her store onto its own online domain: nastygal.com. This rags-to-riches story was a further selling point of Amoruso's 2014 memoir, *#GirlBoss*; another string to her bow alongside an empire that was estimated to reach sales of $300 million in 2015. With such significant sales figures and investments totalling $49 million, she was a hugely inspirational figure to potential entrepreneurs all over the world. Sophia was the figurehead of a movement that had gone from the brand-centric fashion industry to a place where the individual could rise up and succeed.

However, the fairytale was shattered in 2016 when the company filed for bankruptcy alongside lawsuits from previous employees claiming unfair dismissal, mentions of an out-of-touch CEO who had been hired after Amoruso stepped down, and what some employees have called an 'ego explosion' after the launch of the book. The company imploded inwardly while sales slipped and investment went elsewhere. The story that should have continued to inspire and encourage other unconventional and ambitious entrepreneurs to follow their dreams was concluded with a very unhappy ending. While the very limitless nature of the Internet can instil in us a sense of 'anything is possible', perhaps it's also responsible for leading us down unrealistic to unachievable avenues.

When I was studying for my fashion degree, I remember frequently querying what types of jobs I could actually apply for when I graduated. Buyer, marketer or designer were the three generic roles that would spring up, but I wanted to know what else went on behind the scenes of the fashion industry. Five years later and an entirely new set of careers was opened up and slotted into the fashion chain. I've spoken a lot in this book about the numerous changes in the fashion industry recently – to the designers, the owners, the schedules, the routines, the expectations, even the audience – but who is making sure it's all ticking along and continuing to stay afloat behind the scenes? It's easy to say that a brand needs to up their social-media game or that they must frequently change their strategies in order to stay relevant, but who are the people making these things happen?

With these changes and the introduction of the Internet came a whole host of new roles that needed to be filled by skilled individuals. Positions that were only just starting to appear by the time I finished university. Someone was needed to look after the social platforms, another was required to come up with content ideas, while further staff were needed to liaise with bloggers, and on and on it went until the marketing and PR teams of most retailers doubled in size. The web was big business for brands and it took a savvy and specialist new team to make sure it ran as smoothly as possible.

But what it did for a select few was to allow the average Joe, like Amoruso, to build their own fashion businesses from their laptops. The merging of fashion and the Internet led to a new world where you didn't need to know the right people or to have the right status or level of wealth to get started – you could build your own empire, all at the click of a button. The fashion industry was there for the taking and with the right idea, it was anyone's game.

Victoria Beckham

Naomi Campbell

Girlbosses you need to follow

Victoria Beckham

For me, the ultimate girlboss. The lady who manages to look after four children and keep her beautiful home in order all whilst designing and fronting two fashion collections and a best-selling beauty collaboration. She is truly a Wonder Woman.

Chrissy Teigen

Chrissy really doesn't suffer fools gladly, which makes for entertaining viewing on her social channels. But she is also super-successful, the mother of two children and wife to John Legend. She's fun to follow and inspiring to match.

202

Naomi Campbell

Naomi has always been a girlboss in the industry for her world-famous modelling career and uber-confidence. But her charity work – she has founded two charitable organisations, Fashion For Relief and We Love Brazil – is a clear demonstration of her wonderful character.

Chriselle Lim

I talk a little too much about the inspiration I gain from Chriselle. Her content and style are incredible, she always manages to put out new blog and YouTube content and all the while she looks after her two children and maintains a happy marriage.

Karlie Kloss

Seriously, what an inspiring lady. Not only is she the most striking woman I've ever stood next to, she is also so kind-hearted, extremely intelligent and eager to help other females learn and succeed.

Be innovative

Karlie Kloss

#CastMeMarc

'Got what it takes to be the face of Marc
by Marc Jacobs? Marc is casting the FW14 ad
campaign on social! Tag your best modelling
look with #CastMeMarc to enter!'

It's April 2014 and Marc Jacobs posts a photo on his Instagram
feed with this caption. Almost immediately, 70,000 images flood
into the #CastMeMarc hashtag and a social-media frenzy
ensues. The Marc by Marc Jacobs FW14 campaign needs the
freshest new face as its model, and social media is the most
up-to-date and responsive way to find it. Anyone can enter,
from any background, any race, any country, any religion,
and with just a selfie they can win, to become the next big
thing. There are nine winners from the 70,000 entries and

each will be a new face in the first ad campaign for the Marc Jacobs diffusion line. It's a once-in-a-lifetime opportunity that usually only top models would be cast for via the world's most prestigious modelling agencies – and yet you, in your home, sat in your sweat pants, could upload an image of yourself and change your life.

It had never been seen before. Marc Jacobs used the power and reach of social media to dip into the segments of people on the Internet who have something to offer but no idea how to achieve it. These beautiful people were ready and waiting for an opportunity and just needed one chance to unleash their potential.

In November 2016, the campaign was launched for a second time. 'Who will be the next biggest beauty vlogger?' the advert asked, and 31,000 people entered to try their luck for a second time around. This time, just three winners would take part in the #BeautyMarc video series, and after such a huge success with the first campaign, this was the big break that so many were after.

This was the first time that models had been cast in such an informal way, going outside the boundaries of standard modelling circles and into the real world, where there is hidden talent waiting to be found. Social media is now a huge factor in the modelling industry, with the most popular models nurturing social followings of millions. Models are arguably sometimes cast based on how much they're also able to promote the latest collections and catwalk shows – organically (non-contractually), of course. Hence why a number of the most influential bloggers and users in the world are becoming models in their own right.

Marc Jacobs proved that anyone can be a model if they have the right look, democratising fashion and allowing anyone to take part, regardless of who they are and what their background may be.

American Apparel similarly capitalises on the aesthetic of normal people wearing clothing in a more natural and realistic way. And we see it so often on the Instagram pages of beauty brands, where photo after video after photo has been taken by their loyal, make-up savvy fans and re-posted by the brand. The fashion, beauty and social worlds are now so tightly intertwined that they almost rely on each other to grow and prosper. That's why the #CastMeMarc moment was so monumental. The gates were opened for social media to seep into the everyday workings of the (often archaic) fashion industry, and the ordinary outsider could penetrate its shell for the very first time.

Nine models to follow

1. @BellaHadid: Even my Nana probably knows who Bella is, but as one of my favourite ladies in the business, I had to mention her. I find her beauty absolutely astounding.

2. @KaiaGerber: I was once in a lift with Kaia and I didn't even realise at first because I was too busy flapping over my phone. How can someone be so new to catwalk modelling and look like they've done it their whole life?

3. @RomeeStrijd: I love following her beautiful life on Instagram, and she also vlogs her day-to-day routine on her YouTube channel.

4. @Neelamkg: Neelam is going to take the fashion world by storm; she's already making her way there.

5. @AnokYai: I fall in love with every photo I see of Anok. She is truly stunning.

6. @VittoCeretti: Vittoria is someone I'd love to see fronting more campaigns for the biggest brands in the world. I think her look is so unique; she can be transformed in every photo.

7. @Hoskelsa: You could stare at Elsa Hosk all day. She has the most beautiful photos to keep you inspired.

8. @Taylor_Hill: Taylor's popularity exploded around 2015 and she was the face of so many campaigns soon after. Her features are youthful and girly – just beyond beautiful.

9. @Bambilegit: Bambi Northwood Blyth just has one of those gorgeous faces that I love seeing on my feed. She looks like she'd be a lot of fun to hang out with.

Be innovative

Rebecca Minkoff

Rebecca Minkoff leads the connected-store revolution

'It was important for us to create our connected store not for a gimmick or for press, but rather to show our customer we hear her painpoints with brick and mortar shopping and to see what could we do to make her experience offline as good as it has become online.'
Rebecca Minkoff, 2018

I'm a big fan of this new revolution in shopping experiences. That time when Topshop started placing sofas in their stores to form areas to relax in and enjoy — I was all over it. Then there came coffee shops, cupcake stalls, hair salons, tattoo parlours and manicure stations, so you didn't need to leave all day. Stores became experiences, social areas and one-stop shops.

A genius idea if you ask me. But some retailers took the plunge into something even more technologically savvy.

In 2014, Rebecca Minkoff opened her flagship store in New York City. With help from eBay, the store offered a connected online experience within a physical store environment – a hybrid of online shopping with a real-life changing room. Connected Glass shopping walls that act like a touchscreen computer enable customers to browse, select and send items to the changing rooms, with the help of a store assistant. Once inside, various settings allow the customer to adjust the lighting environment of the changing room, and with a built-in connected mirror, the customer can continue to shop the store, ask for new sizes and send items to the till. Or you can pay for them, then and there, via PayPal. It's like shopping online, adding items to your wishlist and sending them to your basket, only with a physical try-on session in between. No more peering around the curtain to ask for another size while trying to cover your dignity.

It's a huge step forward to see online and in-store shopping habits colliding in this way. With microchips placed in the tags of each item, the changing room is able to track which come and go, and which are bought in the interim, providing the brand with in-depth knowledge of which are being tried and not bought (potentially hinting at a fitting issue), and which are being tried and bought faster than others (suggesting that the stores need to call in more stock). Rebecca called it 'fitting-room abandonment' when I spoke to her recently – just like shopping-cart abandonment, but with the stats to see which items were left behind after trying. It's incredibly clever and such a huge innovation for the physical store.

I still remember the days when taking a photograph inside a retail store on your mobile phone was frowned upon. That was until camera phones and WiFi-enabled devices became the norm and phones were being used not only to take quick snaps, but to price compare and research similar items elsewhere. People wanted to spend more time in the store, send pictures of outfit ideas to friends and think about what they were about to buy over a coffee.

This adjustment in the way that consumers shopped in-store and simultaneously online was no doubt the cause of such a rise in connected stores and retail-experience spaces. So a host of other brands caught on. For example, in July 2017, Ted Baker opened their new London store in St Pancras station, with touchscreen signage for customers to shop the latest lookbooks and find styling inspiration while browsing in-store. In 2018, Amazon patented a Smart Mirror that virtually overlays clothing onto a person stood in front of the mirror – so you don't even need to try on any more. And high-street favourite Zara has integrated self-checkout stations within their biggest global store in Madrid.

It even looks like facial recognition may soon become a reality, by which cameras will inform sales staff when a loyal customer walks into their luxury store. I can just imagine a sales associate changing their attitude from welcoming to unbelievably interested when they know a customer with some serious cash to spend just walked in. I'm not overly fond of this innovation – great customer service should be a given, not something for a select few. But digital technologies within stores just seem to be increasing and advancing, with integrated iPads, QR code purchasing, in-store WiFi, touchscreen tables, augmented reality, interactive displays and digital fitting rooms. All integrated into physical stores, in the hope of connecting, enticing and catering to their digital-savvy consumers.

My ideal shopping experience

Imagine you just bought your own store for the first time, and let's say, for the fun of it, that cash is no issue. What would you put into your store to give your customers the best possible experience?

For me, it would be a London store, decorated beautifully to be the ultimate Instagram and Pinterest 'goals'. Somewhere people would want to visit, just because it's so beautiful. There would be a central area with sofas, magazines and coffee-table books, mainly for the partners and friends of the shopper to sit and relax while their other half enjoys their shopping time. Plus, sometimes it's nice to have a sit down while you're shopping. Each sofa would have an iPad (built into the sofa for security) for anyone to browse the lookbooks and website for ideas. And they could order from the sofa if they wish.

In one corner at the front of the store, I would have a little coffee area with a vintage-style coffee machine and healthy, dairy-free snacks. There would be two booths for two groups of four people to sit and enjoy a coffee while browsing the iPad lookbooks, and the barista would be styled in the latest collections. It would also offer takeaway coffees to entice others to venture into the store.

There would be smart mirrors in the changing rooms, as in Rebecca Minkoff's store, to alter the lighting and ambience, as I think that is a game-changer. Bad lighting can put you off even the most amazing clothing. There would be little velvet seats inside each changing room, too, because I love to be able to sit sometimes, and the changing rooms would be beautifully designed for the best possible mirror-selfie opportunity. Because why would brands want to miss out on free promotion? The smart mirrors would also allow you to see if other colours and sizes of your item are available within the store. And at the end of your try-on, you can have your items bagged up for you in the changing areas before you exit the store.

How cool would it be to have digital screens next to blocks of clothing on the walls, with everything on the walls linked to that screen? You can flick through the catalogue and see what the stylists have matched with the items in front of you and how you could wear it. You could add the items you love to your changing room and in-store assistant stylists would round them up and take them to the changing room for you, saving you having to walk around with countless items hanging from the crook of your arm. If you lived in London and had spent over £600, you could then have the items bagged up and couriered to your home anywhere within the city.

Next to the exit of the store there would be an iPad to send your ideas and feedback. This is one of the best ways to get your customer service levels on point, to change up your stock, clean up your store environment or find out things you wouldn't otherwise be privy to.

So that's my dream store. What's yours?

January 2016

33 Virtual models in starring roles

Are you even cool any more if you're not CGI? Instagrammers probably thought their biggest competition were the people around them on a similar number of followers. But actually, the people that brands are looking to dress in their latest apparel aren't people at all. They're CGI models – airbrushed, flawless and dressed in the latest Chanel bouclé jacket. Miquela of @Lilmiquela has over 1.1 million followers, has been featured in fashion mags including *V* magazine, *Paper* and *Foam*, and on the cover of *King Kong* magazine. She's designed clothing for various brands and retailers and has been cast as a model in a number of campaigns. And she's a CGI 19-year-old, 'living in LA'.

Shudu Gram

But Miquela is not alone. Shudu of @shudu.gram has over 130,000 followers, and an Instagram profile that describes her as the 'world's first digital supermodel'. Shudu was designed by British photographer Cameron-James Wilson as an art project and a 'virtual celebration of beautiful, dark-skinned women'. And her popularity boomed when Rihanna's Fenty Beauty reposted a photo of Shudu 'wearing' their vibrant orange lipstick on their Instagram page to millions. The social world went crazy — both positively and negatively, of course, but it was something we just hadn't seen before: CGI models taking the place of real people and competing for air time. Have we gotten to a stage where we're so fed up of real people that we're looking for the next best thing? Scary, scary thought.

It's no wonder that virtual-reality models are becoming so popular, when even the most luxurious of fashion houses are eager to champion new digital faces. In 2016, Louis Vuitton printed their latest campaign imagery, starring Lightning, the pink-haired Final Fantasy XIII character. In the imagery, she stands, arms outstretched, with a Louis Vuitton clutch dangling from her virtual fingertips. And in the video, she jumps around like only a computer-game character could, in leather jackets and cleated-sole Louis Vuitton shoes to an epic Final Fantasy soundtrack. I'd be lying if I said I didn't do a double take when I spotted a CGI fantasy character with a Louis Vuitton logo emblazoned across the same page. But I must admit, I love it. It's modern, it's forward-thinking and it's aiming at a youthful audience. Why not try something new? Louis Vuitton are established enough to be able to try something once and run the risk of it being a major flop, but then the press alongside it would be enough to garner a new audience anyway, so really it's a win-win.

It's an interesting development when elsewhere the industry is beginning to champion inclusivity and diversity and promote the message that non-airbrushed skin and flaws are part of someone's natural beauty. And then we have such models being cast aside and replaced by 'new-gen influencers' who can be dressed, airbrushed and created to be exactly what a brand envisions for their imagery. Food for thought.

When CGI went mainstream

A few more examples of how CGI has been embraced by the fashion world:

- ○ Aimi Eguchi: Aimi Eguchi was found to be a CGI singer within the popular Japanese girlband AKB 48, after building a fanbase who believed she was entirely real. In fact, she was composited from the facial features of six other members of the band.

- ○ Bermuda: @bermudaisbae, is another CGI influencer, who posted a 'collab' pic with Lil Miquela to show that they're sticking together as CGI stars ...

- ○ Blawko: @blawko22 is the first male CGI fashion influencer, complete with face tattoos and a badass attitude, who started an Instagram drama with Bermuda because of something she 'said' about Lil Miquela. What on earth am I even writing? Either way, the creators of these CGI influencers are smart cookies and seem to be working together for world domination.

- ○ Marc Jacobs: Lightning wasn't the first time that Louis Vuitton had dabbled in CGI characters. Their former artistic director Marc Jacobs designed costumes for the virtual Japanese popstar Hatsune Miku in 2013.

- Alexander McQueen: It wasn't CGI, but it was one of the first times we saw non-human models on the catwalks. During the famous 2006 Alexander McQueen show in Paris, set to a haunting string soundtrack, Kate Moss was pictured in hologram at the end of the show.

- Pat McGrath: Due to Lil Miquela sharing her 'virtual looks' on her Instagram, she became one of Pat McGrath's new faces, the #McGrathMuses, in February 2018, alongside the likes of Naomi Campbell and Hailey Baldwin.

- Prada: In February 2018, Lil Miquela 'attended' the Prada show in Milan and was handed their Instagram account to take over.

Be innovative

Alexander McQueen A/W06

Be the first to adapt

The world is moving quickly and the best thing to do is accept it and move with it, before everyone else strides ahead. There's always something new happening online, in the social feeds or even in the mainstream, and it's those of us who are open to the changes and who embrace them straight away that will benefit the most. The innovators who are first to cause a scene and create a movement are the ones to take all the praise and reach above the noise of the industry. Whether that's by embracing technology, understanding and moving with the changes in the fashion world, respecting new faces, being inspired by the latest crazes, supporting new routines or challenging the status quo of an industry that could become stagnated. The first bloggers on the scene back in 2006 are still extremely popular and respected for a reason; they saw the potential and jumped on it immediately. Adapting to the ever-changing environment is paramount to staying ahead of the fashion game.

Be the first to adapt

Cat Meffan

Fitness got trendy

Every time I go to LA, I get this urge to do yoga, find the nearest protein-smoothie café and walk around in capri leggings and a Sweaty Betty sports bra. The majority of people in Hollywood seem to strut around in amazing sportswear, either heading to or walking home from the local yoga studio, barre, Pilates class or spin session. And why ever not, when the weather is incredible 99 per cent of the time and you don't need to wear a jacket, or jeans for that matter. Seeing so many healthy, motivated people strolling around the streets with a water bottle in hand is so inspiring; it gives you the urge to work out and be a better version of yourself.

Twenty years ago, the number of places to buy gymwear or leggings for your step class, especially for women, was pretty slim. If you wanted to flex like Mr Motivator, you went to Nike, Adidas, Umbro, Puma, Reebok, Ellesse, Kappa – those big sports brands that catered for everyone and anyone. There

Carly Rowena

were no specialist stores for beautifully designed yoga apparel or Pilates leggings, because at the time it was nowhere near as popular as it is today. I remember when yoga blew up in the UK, and suddenly everyone wanted to be bendy, lean and super-stretched-out. I think it was Madonna that kicked off the craze in 2003, aged 45, when she showed off her lean and super-flexible bod in the 'Hollywood' music video. After that, fitness got trendy. It was cool to be a gym bunny, it was praised to look after your health and inspiration for your daily workout was everywhere you looked.

The need for a healthy lifestyle became mainstream – and thankfully so. I look back with eye rolls on those days when you would go to clubs and come home stinking of second-hand cigarette smoke, or worse, with cigarette burns in your dress. The scientific information and news coverage regarding health and fitness just wasn't what it is now. Fewer people were vegetarian, more people smoked, vegans were looked upon as 'hippies' and unhealthy fad diets came and went. But now, often you're the odd one out if you still tuck into a steak on a night out. Vegan restaurants are popping up everywhere in the cities for those interested in eating clean. People are better educated and aware of the detrimental effects of the meat and the dairy industry on their health and the environment, and they're making huge lifestyle changes to address this.

This emphasis on healthy living and the desire to feel amazing is fuelling a big business – an even bigger business than it was. The likes of Lulu Lemon and Sweaty Betty (who both launched in 1998), Varley, Victoria's Secret, Under Armour, Gym Shark and the sportswear lines of high-street and luxury brands have invaded the space and got us all kitted out in stunning stretchy Lycra of every colour and pattern. Fitness-wear has become an enormous fashion business, especially for women. Sometimes I feel sexier in a sports bra and tight-fitting leggings than I do in a pair of jeans. No wonder the LA ladies love to walk to the shops in their capris.

But it's not just the fashion business who have capitalised on it – it's the smoothie-maker brands, the vegan cookbooks, the sneakers industry, the gym owners, the private spin-class instructors, the fitness Instagrammers, the personal trainers, the soya and avocado farmers. They've all had a boost. We all want our avo toast before a spin class, and to be dressed in Sweaty Betty leggings, drinking a protein smoothie as we saunter home, shaking our tight tushes.

How to jump on the fitness bandwagon

The fitness hype is everywhere – magazines, advertisements and now it's all over your social-media feed. So why not embrace it, and enjoy all the free inspiration?

If you're getting into fitness for the first time and you're daunted by classes or the gym, I'd firstly say, you have no need to worry. Many people are in a similar position to you. In the gym, everyone is thinking about themselves – their day, their schedule and to-do list – rather than what you might look like attempting this yoga class for the first time. Plus, who cares? You're there for you, not them. But if you are still concerned, find a friend to go along with you.

The fitness bandwagon is gathering pace for a reason. Everyone wants to feel and look their best, and buying yourself some gorgeous activewear really does help to kick-start your enthusiasm. My motivation to work out goes up tenfold if I have a new piece of clothing to wear. So treat yourself to some flattering sportswear and find a fitness class or regime that you absolutely love. As I mentioned in my plan for my dream shopping street (see page 25), I love Nike, Adidas, Sweaty Betty, Varley and Lulu Lemon – all the usual suspects – for my fitness-wear.

And for that extra inspo, here are a few fitness ladies from the UK that I'm always inspired by, who look healthy and fit and often wear the best sportswear going:

@carlyrowena

The most genuinely gorgeous person inside and out, with a heart of gold and abs of steel. She is constantly in gymwear and offers loads of workout advice and videos, so you're bound to feel inspired.

@catmeffan

A yoga babe with one of the most amazing fitness wardrobes you will ever see. Plus, her yoga videos make me wish I was far more bendy.

@aliceliveing

One of the loveliest ladies I've ever met, with a healthy, toned physique, great fitness videos for beginners and even her own line of fitness-wear, among the rest of her comfy fitness wardrobe.

@gracefituk

One of those ladies who has worked hard for her figure, has a bum you could only dream of owning and doesn't take life too seriously. She inspires you without making you feel too guilty for eating cake.

@sjanaelise

The most flexible yoga lady from Australia, with the biggest smile and an even larger heart – Sjana and I wandered around Japan together in 2015 and I've been inspired by her travels and yoga poses ever since.

Be the first to adapt

Netflix merchandise gets hyped

Remember the days when band tees were the coolest thing ever? Or maybe I just thought they were. I definitely have Metallica, Gaslight Anthem and Bruce Springsteen tees in my chest of drawers for the days I fancy being cool again. And I still love wearing them, not only because I love these bands, but because it's a way to outwardly show your music tastes and personality to those people passing you by. (When I was younger, it was one of my favourite ways to attract the male species, hoping that another music fan might spot me in a crowd and we would fall in love listening to the *Born in the USA* album. LOL.)

That premise still exists, only now it's moved on to slogan tees, merchandise and your favourite quote on a hoodie — all inspired by online influences. Netflix streaming became

Be the first to adapt

Louis Vuitton S/S18

available in Europe in January 2012 and our lives have never been the same. Hours upon hours of binge fests on your favourite Netflix show can happen at the touch of a laptop button. And with that obsession has come the desire for merchandise that outwardly shows you're the biggest fan in the world.

Stranger Things, for example – hello, cash cow! Topshop created a full collection of *Stranger Things* apparel for Halloween 2017 in time for the arrival of Season two. Very, very clever. Of course, it was a sell-out. Fans couldn't wait to wear tees, hoodies, jackets, bags and everything else emblazoned with slogans, imagery and that famous retro red logo. Hence why Target, Etsy, TruffleShuffle, Amazon and Hot Topic all got in on the action, too.

We have meme quotes on T-shirts, fashion-week shows using soundtracks from Netflix programmes and even Disney characters splattered over Vans trainers. Even luxury brands are integrating mainstream pop-culture influences into their collections. Louis Vuitton incorporating a *Stranger Things*

T-shirt into their runway show, Coach collaborating with Disney, Moschino designing both a Barbie and Looney Tunes collection – these collaborations are childish and gimmicky, but mixed with higher price points and well-loved luxury brands, the juxtaposition makes the items instant bestsellers for those nostalgic adults.

People love it – to wear a piece of apparel that displays our adoration for our favourite TV show or Disney character, or even to make a political statement with a perfectly worded quotation. You don't even need to speak any more, when your T-shirt can summarise your mood or your interests in just one statement.

My favourite luxury x mainstream collabs

1. Adidas x *Dragon Ball*
2. Moschino x Barbie
3. Louis Vuitton x *Stranger Things*
4. Dior x Chimamanda Ngozi Adichie quotation
5. Louis Vuitton x *Final Fantasy*
6. Moschino x Looney Tunes
7. Coach x Disney
8. Bobby Abley x Power Rangers
9. Vans x Disney

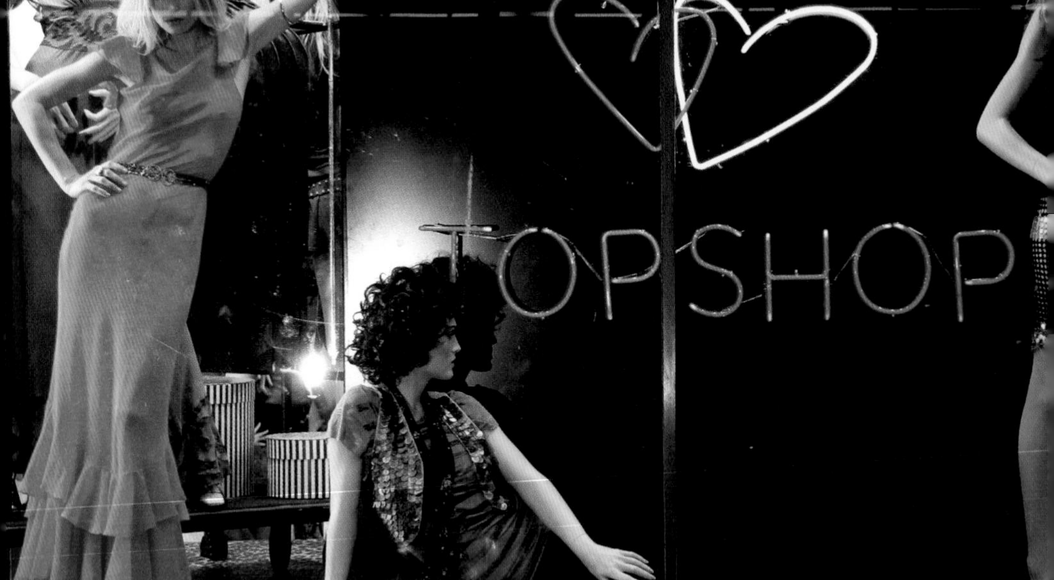
kate moss
TOPSHOP

March 2013

The influencers design the collections

The UK youth market went crazy in 2013 when River Island announced their collaboration with singer and superstar Rihanna to co-design her own clothing collection. Brands have worked with celebrities for years, garnering the power of their popularity, respect and recognition to elevate the sales of new products, but design collaborations were rare up until this point. I'm sure you recall the sell-out Kate Moss for Topshop collaboration in 2010 – and if not, I can assure you it was one of the most coveted collections in fashion at the time. For the Rihanna collection, River Island's sales grew by 4 per cent and the influence of such collaborative partnerships was once again solidified.

Subsequently and consequently, the market has seen the collaboration of many other celebrities, models and artists with huge worldwide brands. Beyoncé worked with Topshop to develop Ivy Park Sportswear, Rihanna worked with Chopard jewellery on a capsule collection, model Jourdan Dunn developed the Londunn range with Missguided and a variety of beauty gurus have worked with the likes of Too Faced, Mac and Becca Cosmetics on hugely successful beauty lines. There is little need for proof of the success of social star collaborations when Kim Kardashian released her KKW beauty line to earn $14 million in sell-out product sales. It is no longer solely the creative directors and lead designers in fashion houses who are offering input into the clothing we wear each season.

But we have also seen social creators branching out on their own, developing beauty lines and clothing ranges under their own social branding. Leandra Medine Cohen of Man

Be the first to adapt

Chiara Ferragni Collection S/S16

Aimee Song

Repeller created her blog in 2012 and by 2016 had designed her own line of footwear, MR by Man Repeller, exclusive to Net-A-Porter. Jenn Im, popular fashion YouTuber and Instagrammer, launched Eggie in 2017. Julie Sariñana of Sincerely Jules launched a clothing collection of the same name and Aimee Song of Song of Style created Two Songs with her sister Dani, all with a cool LA vibe. Samantha Maria, popular UK YouTuber and blogger, also designed her own line of off-duty stylish apparel branded Novem & Knight, while Alexandra Pereira of Lovely Pepa built her own brand and collection, again under her own branding.

Zoe Sugg of Zoella was the first YouTube creator in the UK to launch her own line, with Zoella Beauty, adding Zoella branded travel bags, bath melts and shower gels to the shelves of every Superdrug store around the UK. They sold like wildfire – in fact, they broke Superdrug sales records, selling out in just one day. Zoe went on to create Zoella Lifestyle, adding candles, cushions and adorable homeware accessories to her list of own-name products and has since sold 10 million units of Zoella branded products around the world.

But arguably the most successful creator fashion line is that of Italian blogger Chiara Ferragni. The Chiara Ferragni Collection launched in 2013, offering a line of shoes and accessories with a recognisable shape and design that became so successful they grew to a stockist list of over 300 stores worldwide and reportedly reached revenues of $7.5 million in 2016. It's also clear that Chiara's audience really adore her taste in shoes, given that in 2014 she influenced the sales of 16,000 pairs in two weeks during a collaboration range with Steve Madden. And some people say that bloggers and 'influencers' are just a phase?

So where is it going, and what's next? While some of the largest bloggers in the industry have diverted their attention to their own clothing lines, and a number of bloggers have collaborated with brands on their own collections, there is still space for so many more creatives to leave their mark. Compared to how many bloggers there are in the space, the number of creators who have moved into developing their own fashion label is actually very small. I, for one, would love to see what other creators come up with. You never know, maybe one day I'll be among this list. The biggest bloggers are often those with an amazing sense of fashion, confidence to wear anything they like and an eye for putting looks together. I'm always so inspired to try something new, because I've seen an item on an Instagram profile I follow. So why wouldn't we as an audience not want to buy into that, and wear items the bloggers have created themselves? It seems like a no-brainer to me.

If I designed my own brand . . .

I've never spoken about this openly before, but seeing as you picked up this book, I'm willing to share a lot more with you here than I have before. That's the beauty of this book!

I would love to design my own fashion label. When I was 14, I remember sitting in my kitchen and chatting with my step-dad about potential brand names for my fashion line. I bought this incredible, super-heavy book called *Colors for Modern Fashion* by Nancy Riegelman – I highly recommend it if you want to learn how to draw fashion illustrations. And it makes an insane coffee-table book. Buying that kicked off my dream to start my own label. Since then, I (unknowingly) created another brand – this one: Inthefrow. But to add on a line of products under a similar or the same name is a dream of mine. And so many wonderful people who follow me have often asked why I haven't yet launched a clothing line.

So what would I design if I did do this? I want to create clothing that I would personally wear and love every single day. The kind of things I want to find in the stores but just can't because the exact style isn't quite right for me. Items that fit my own style and vibe to a tee. So there would of course be a range of suits, incredible knits, trousers for every occasion, the perfect white tee, silk shift dresses and classic jackets. Everything I wear now but with my own take on it.

Wish me luck!

Cara photobombs the runway

It's a cold day in February for London Fashion Week and the Giles Deacon show is about to hit lift-off. The lights come up, the music starts and the hottest model of the moment, Cara Delevingne, takes to the catwalk with her phone in hand as she struts down the runway towards the paps. She holds her phone up in selfie mode as she records live from the runway, capturing six videos on her phone that she will later post on her Instagram page. I wish I could say I was there to see it. I wasn't, but at least I saw all the coverage afterwards as the fashion world went into overdrive.

The catwalk and the surrounding aisles of buyers, journalists and fashion figureheads had always been a place for business, formalities and structure. On that day, the social space invaded the walls of the fashion institution and

showed how relevant and essential it was for the modern age in the industry. The brand was harnessing the power of Cara's audience to promote their show, and Cara was showing how badass the team at Giles Deacon were for allowing her to bring tech and her audience onto the catwalk. It was a first, and the closest anyone had been to the models on the runway in the history of the modern fashion show.

Today, we are in a place where livestreaming by the audience in the frow has become the norm, and Instagram Stories, Periscope, Snapchat, Facebook Live and Instagram Live now offer immediate, non-filtered, non-edited coverage from frow to viewer. Before this, it was only when *Vogue*, *Elle* or any of the other mass fashion magazines printed their favourite looks from the spring/summer or autumn/winter runways that the general consumer would get a glimpse of next season's trends and garments.

The four walls of the catwalk show were only to be seen by fashion's most prestigious journalists, marketeers and buyers, and retained as a well-kept secret until the print magazines were published. That was until bloggers and online journalists – with their seconds of lead time from photograph to posting – took a seat at the shows and the world could see the runway looks as they happened.

Previously, though, in January 2007, Giorgio Armani had broadcast his collection live on the web; the first time this had ever been seen in the world of haute couture. Later, in 2010, Burberry would erect a full camera rig at their runway shows to record the catwalk from alternative angles and provide a 3D livestream for those watching via events around the globe. Topshop Unique were next to jump on board and stream the show to their customers live on the Topshop website. Fast-forward to 2018, and there is now a plethora of brands bringing their live shows directly to the homes of their audience. If you watched the Victoria Beckham show for A/W18, you may have spotted me in the frow, directly in the firing line of the video camera next to the model's entranceway. In the new media age, there is a fly on the wall at every catwalk show, inside every backstage area and in the hands of every front-row guest. The fashion world has nowhere to hide.

The fashion shows that changed how I saw fashion

Burberry

I had only dreamed of attending a fashion-week show when I was at university, and yet here in my hands was an invitation to the S/S16 Burberry show in London. I had never felt prouder of where I had taken my blog than I did in that moment. And if anything, it only elevated my love for this brand. The first year I attended, I was in the fourth row; the following year I was in the frow. Dreams really can come true with some hard work and determination.

Dior

As someone who dotes on this brand, a ticket to the A/W17 Dior show was beyond my wildest dreams. I was wearing head-to-toe Dior, sitting front row at the second Maria Grazia show in Paris and I felt a wave of emotion hit me. I couldn't believe I

Victoria Beckham A/W17

was there, to see the brand-new Dior collections in real time. The clothes were given a story, an energy and a personality. I was totally speechless.

Giorgio Armani

As someone who adores Giorgio Armani beauty, I was initially drawn to the make-up via my love of the fashion brand. Mr Armani is such a pioneer and figurehead. His work demands so much respect within the industry and I felt so honoured to be seated at his show for the first time for S/S17. Within those four walls, there was a feeling, and a vibration, that it was going to be something special.

Julien Macdonald

A ticket to a Julien Macdonald show is a ticket to a good time. His shows are often late in the day's schedule because they set you up for a dance party. The music, the energy, the fast pace and, of course, the exquisite, embellished, lavish collections are unlike anything you could ever imagine. Every year, since S/S15, Julien's shows in London are a highlight for me.

Victoria Beckham

I remember so clearly when I was offered a seat at the A/W17 Victoria Beckham show. I texted my best friend instantly — the one person I knew would be even more excited than I was. I adore Victoria's designs, as they mirror my love of tailoring, clean lines and sophisticated silhouettes. That show blew me away and it was a moment when I actually felt like I had a real place in the fashion industry.

GLAMOUR

www.glamour.com

DECEMBER 2015

Christmas. Cracked!

448
genius presents

382
sexiest party looks ever

Plus...
Christmas with Katy Perry

We sent a sex writer to a convent
What could possibly go wrong?

The rise of the super-vlogger

Tanya Burr

First stop YouTube,
now the
world

PLUS
How you can meet her!

The rudest question *all* women get asked
And 12 kick-ass ways to shut it down

The super-bloggers get the gig

Standing in your local supermarket, you glance over the magazines in the racks for something that takes your fancy. You recognise your favourite actresses, that singer from *The X-Factor* and maybe Ryan Gosling looking fantastic on the cover of *GQ*, but then you spy Tanya Burr looking sultry and glamorous on the cover of *Glamour* magazine. It's December 2015, and a YouTuber (that's a noun now) just got the front cover of a fashion monthly. Tanya has an audience of over 5 million, so it's no surprise that *Glamour* wanted a piece of her pie. And it figures — her front cover increased their year-on-year sales figures by a whopping 17 per cent.

But Tanya is not alone in rocking the status quo of the traditional media world. In April of the same year, Chiara Ferragni of The Blonde Salad, the uber-successful Italian blogger and entrepreneur, was the very first blogger to land the front cover of *Vogue* Spain and has since graced 26 magazine covers around the world. For (arguably) the most famous fashion magazine in the world to place a blogger, rather than a model, actress or artist, on their cover is a sign of just how relevant and important bloggers and influencers have become to the fashion industry. For an institution such as *Vogue* to acknowledge the influence of a fashion blogger was a huge step forward towards a cross-over of these two mediums. No longer did the two have to be separate; they could garner the power of the other to grow simultaneously. A blogger could be taken as seriously as a musician or an actress without being a world-famous supermodel.

Yet, the modelling industry is creating influential faces of its own. The most celebrated models in 2017 were Insta-famous, influential social-media figures and were therefore also seen regularly in the traditional press. Gigi Hadid hosts an Instagram audience of over 40 million, her sister Bella over 18 million and Cara Delevingne 41 million. These models walk the Victoria's Secret show, grace the billboard advertisements of the biggest brands in the world and walk for the most coveted designers at fashion week. But even then, there is a shift appearing, with brands selecting bloggers and social-media figures to feature alongside, or instead of, their huge ambassadors. L'Oréal Paris created a buzz in 2016 when they signed Swiss fashion blogger Kristina Bazan to their roster of spokeswomen, alongside Karlie Kloss, Cheryl Cole and Helen Mirren. Later they would also create the L'Oréal Beauty Squad, a group of five female bloggers and YouTubers, to become ambassadors for the brand throughout the year — myself included in this original roster of five, which was later increased to eight.

The shift is apparent, and the results are measurable. The biggest and most respected bloggers and social faces in the industry are breaking their way into the fashion world, often meeting unexpectedly open arms. And rightly so; they are influencing brand choices, the things we buy and the places we visit. Tanya's front cover was not only a brilliant opportunity for *Glamour*, it was a statement that the super-bloggers are becoming a fashion force to be reckoned with. In March 2018, *Glamour* went live again with not only one blogger on the cover, but three separate covers adorned by three social superstars: Zoe Sugg, Huda Kattan and Patricia Bright.

The stars are now not only on the covers, but inside them. YouTuber Jim Chapman began working as a contributing writer for *GQ* in 2016 and the likes of Charlotte Tilbury and Kate Moss began working as contributing editors at *Vogue* when Edward Enninful became editor in chief. I also became a contributing fashion columnist for *Glamour* when they launched their bi-annual magazines and began to focus on online content. And we now have *Blogosphere* magazine, which is dedicated to the blogging industry and is successfully selling thousands of magazines displaying influential faces on their cover. I was so proud to be invited as a cover star in September 2016, and the magazine has gone from strength to strength since then. It looks like interest in the industry isn't dwindling just yet.

The cross-over between social stars, celebrities and artists in the fashion and beauty world has brought down the iron gates of the fashion industry and made it much more inclusive and diverse.

Be the first to adapt

The coolest things bloggers have achieved

○ Magazine front covers. Hundreds of them now. From Camila Coelho covering *Elle* Brazil not once but twice, as well as *Women's Health* and *InStyle*, to Nicole Warne of Gary Pepper Girl on the cover of *Elle* Australia, Chiara Ferragni for *Vogue* Spain and *Vogue* Turkey, Tanya Burr for *Glamour* UK and Zoe Sugg of Zoella on the cover of *Glamour* and *Cosmopolitan*.

○ #DGMillennials. A chance for new faces and influences to shine, walking the catwalk in the newest collections for Dolce & Gabbana. Swapping out popular model faces for social-media stars with millions of followers and burgeoning talent could have been met with mixed reviews, but it only elevated the Dolce & Gabbana brand even more. Especially among the younger generations. The likes of Cameron Dallas, Jude Law's son Rafferty Law, Cindy Crawford's son Presley Gerber and Pamela Anderson's sons Dylan Jagger and Brandon Thomas Lee were among the huge line-up of fresh talent. And it was an enormous success, leading to a number of further millennial-casted shows.

○ Charity work. Claire Marshall, based in LA and the coolest fashion and beauty YouTuber I've been lucky enough to meet, raised $35,000 in donations for charity Pencils of Promise, from the sales of her own custom T-shirts, enabling the building of a three-classroom school in Mafi Mediage, Ghana, that will impact the lives of 918 students over the following years.

○ Collaborating on fashion lines. Arielle of Something Navy and Cupcakes and Cashmere's Emily Schuman have both designed their own sell-out fashion collections with Nordstrom. Chriselle Lim worked with J.O.A. to design a line of summer-inspired clothing that led on to a second collection months later. And I was lucky enough to launch a line of curated bags with Strathberry in 2018.

39

Burberry redefines the rules of the catwalk

The room went quiet, with only mutterings audible over the live musicians opening the show for the Burberry A/W16 collection. The frow is eager to feast their eyes on the latest pieces and video cameras are rigged in every corner of the room to capture the catwalk show for the masses viewing at home. This is the first time ever that Burberry is unveiling their 'see-now-buy-now' runway collection. The name is pretty self-explanatory: customers can buy the items they see on the catwalk, right now, to wear for the appropriate season. No waiting around for six months like Burberry had offered in previous seasons with a pre-order system. If you liked what you saw on the catwalk, you could buy it immediately online, and wear it tomorrow. Or near enough. It was a fashion revolution.

Burberry A/W16

This new method creates a huge shift in seasonality for products and abolishes the pomp and circumstance of the original runway show. The concept is based around giving customers the products at the time when their inspiration and interest in them is at their highest. Why would anyone want to wait six months to get their hands on them? And yet, that is the way the fashion industry currently ticks, keeping us eagerly waiting for items to drop into the online store after their unveiling months before. Now, Burberry and a number of other brands are giving us the 'In-season drop', and it's making fashion faster and more responsive than ever.

Potentially too fast for Tom Ford, who after two seasons as a SNBN show reverted back to the original model. Apparently, sales were lower than the previous season and the timings weren't aligning. The same goes for Thakoon, who, after trying the new model, found that sales were not as hoped and therefore decided to hit pause on his forward-thinking strategy. It would seem that in some cases, the retail environment isn't quite ready.

Yet there are still brands willing to try the direct-to-consumer model, favouring the 'I want what I want when I want it' generation, according to consumer psychologist Kit Yarrow. I couldn't have put it better myself, and I'm certainly one of those people who would buy the products off the runway model's back given the chance. Mulberry have also joined the crew, skipping their September 2017 show to gear up for the see-now-buy-now model in February 2018. Being at that show and knowing that I could buy the cool new bag in the hands of the model right then and there was such a modern and exciting twist to the fashion-week routine.

There is no more wanting and wishing, just inspiring and purchasing – right here, right now. The audience sitting at home, watching the catwalk show on their iPhone, can immediately click to buy the items that make them swoon and have them delivered to their home with next-day delivery. With live-streaming, Instastories and play-by-play social posts, the runway has become accessible to the masses, and shoppable by all.

Whether we will see the majority of fashion brands transitioning to a see-now-buy-now model is hard to say, especially given the few recent set-backs. But if it does become hugely successful for the other brands partaking, it could be the unexpected breaking of the fashion-week cycle. It's a totally different format to the way it always used to be, and it is all thanks to the web and direct purchasing. Ask yourself this: if you see it on Instagram today, do you want to buy it now, or in six months' time?

Burberry S/S16

Be Social

Tommy Hilfiger S/S18

The fashion brands you can see now and buy now

Here is a list of the brands that have implemented a see-now-buy-now approach in the last two years, just in case you wanted to get spendy while you're watching at home! Some of the brands have only dabbled, such as Prada and Louis Vuitton, offering just a few items for sale directly after the show. In fact, a large number of brands appear to be trying this technique rather than transitioning entirely. It will be interesting to keep an eye on these brands over the next few seasons to see whether they continue to adopt such a forward-thinking strategy and if some move to a full buy-now format.

Alexander Wang
Anya Hindmarch
Baja East
Burberry
Coach
Club Monaco
Kate Spade
Louis Vuitton
Mansur Gavriel
Michael Kors
Misha Nonoo
Moschino
Mulberry

Nicopanda
Oliver Spencer
Rachel Zoe
Ralph Lauren
Rebecca Minkoff
Tommy Hilfiger
Topshop Unique
Urban Zen
Victoria's Secret
Vivienne Westwood
Yeezy
Zadig & Voltaire

Susie bursts the fashion bubble

The blogging industry is huge. There are thousands of bloggers, covering topics from interiors to vehicles, travel, fashion and food, who have grown audiences of millions and who work with the biggest brands in the world. But it was when *Vogue* published an online discussion piece where the Creative Digital Director of *Vogue* US, Sally Singers, boldly instructed bloggers to 'find another business', that the blogging industry realised they had reached a new level of success – where their businesses were threatening even the most elite, global fashion institutions.

Susie Lau

'It seems to be all about turning up, looking
ridiculous, posing, twitching in your seat as
you check your social media feeds, fleeing,
changing, repeating . . . It's all pretty
embarrassing.'
Alessandra Codinha, Vogue.com Fashion News
Editor, September 2016

It was the round up of Milan Fashion Week 2016, and four of
Vogue's US editors were discussing the shows, all whilst writing
openly and critically about their feelings towards fashion
bloggers attending the events. The majority of bloggers sat
back in shock, while a confident few were eager to voice their
disappointment in the writers they had once admired. One of
those was Susie Lau, author of the globally recognised fashion
blog Style Bubble. She wrote:

'The fashion establishment don't want
their circles enlarged, and for the ivory
tower to remain forever that: towering and
impenetrable.'

But it would appear that the ivory towers of *Vogue* were starting
to wobble as a new generation of fashion writers – who could

Susie Lau

single-handedly capture audiences on a scale of hundreds of thousands – started to be ushered into those front-row seats. A media frenzy ensued, with Instagrammers, bloggers, tweeters and mainstream media commenting on the story that was acknowledging (for what felt like the first time) the tension between traditional journalists and the world of new-media bloggers. There had always been a silent rivalry between the two since the first bloggers came onto the scene and started stepping into the shoes of those who were there first. But never before had either party spoken so openly about the situation, and certainly not with such scorn. Shea Marie of Peace Love Shea didn't take the matter lightly. She spoke out to her 1 million followers and boldly retorted:

'I'm sorry if you can't accept that what a "public figure" wears on the street is undoubtedly more influential than your post-fashion week column. That the fashion world isn't controlled by you alone anymore.'

I would imagine that she was voicing what a lot of the fashion bloggers were quietly thinking.

It was as though the *Vogue* writers didn't realise just how many people would be offended by their remarks. Or perhaps they thought the article wouldn't be read by the people that mattered? Or perhaps, and I feel this is the likely answer, they just wanted to cause a storm in a teacup. That one day in Milan had just become too much for them and they couldn't wait to get it down on paper . . . or online, for thousands to see and further tens of thousands to share. With hindsight, this feels like a nervous, jealous conversation between ladies over dinner that should have stayed between the four walls of the Italian restaurant.

Be the first to adapt

Sally Singers wrote:

'Note to bloggers who change head-to-toe paid-
to-wear outfits every hour: please stop. Find
another business. You are heralding the death
of style.'

The bloggers were right to be offended. But the magazine
directors, writers and editors were right to be concerned. Those
in the digital space reach their audience instantly, sharing
content from catwalk to Instastory and in some cases gathering
much larger viewing figures than *Vogue* or any other magazine
could dream of. They are sitting in the front row because of the
influence they own and the content they produce. And while
industry staples such as *Vogue* will always have an integral part
to play in the fashion industry, I think they may need to accept
that there are some new players in town who are becoming just
as influential as the words they write for their magazines.

Shini Park

Sandra Hagelstam

15 of the most innovative fashion bloggers

The fashion blogging space is vast and filled with some truly incredible writers, stylists, directors and creatives. So many have pushed the industry forward, whether in their style or their creative flair, or just for trying something new and innovating the space. Below are the bunch that I feel have moved the blogging industry to new heights and accelerated the movement:

1. Susie Lau: Style Bubble

2. Chriselle Lim: The Chriselle Factor

3. Sandra Hagelstam: 5 Inch and Up

4. Chiara Ferragni: The Blonde Salad

5. Margaret Zhang: Margaret Zhang

6. Kristina Bazan: Kayture

7. Shini Park: Park & Cube

8. Leandra Medine Cohen: Man Repeller

9. Garance Doré: Atelier Doré

10. Scott Schuman: The Sartorialist

11. Nicole Warne: Gary Pepper Girl

12. Aimee Song: Song of Style

13. Julie Sariñana: Sincerely Jules

14. Rumi Neeley: Fashion Toast

15. Samantha Maria: Samantha Maria

Last thoughts

Technology has been the driving force behind the huge changes we have seen within the fashion industry over the last 20 years. But a lot of the change has come from us – the population, the people adoring, living and inspiring the fashion industry. Attitudes have shifted and people are standing up for the things that they believe in, spurred on by the reach and conversations happening within social media. Allowing the ordinary person a platform from which to voice their concerns and injustices has enabled everyone to push forward for change.

Be culturally aware and diverse. I have only touched on a few moments in this book: #TimesUp, plus-size models, the abolition of fur and the movement to become not only more diverse and inclusive, but to reach a stage where those words aren't needed any more, where everyone is living in a world of equal opportunities. They are all issues that have been spoken of before, but not loudly enough that it would ever make a difference. With social platforms, everyone has a voice, everyone has an opinion and there's no way to muffle the noise. Awareness is growing because we have all used our voices.

But we must stay attuned to everything that is happening within this industry. Be aware of the impacts – not only to improve our understanding of the fashion industry's inner workings, but to protect the fashion world, and the physical world, which we adore.

Fast fashion and product wastage, the dying high street, our lack of browsing privacy and the issues with counterfeiting – the more we learn about the impacts of our consumerism, the better we can continue to protect and enjoy our favourite industry. The better we can be as human beings.

Be innovative. Be individuals. Wear what you like, live how you like and gain inspiration from every corner of the physical and digital world. The most successful people in this industry got to their position because they had an idea, thrived on inspiration and believed in their abilities. Believe in your own skills, your own ideas and take the lead. And Be the first to adapt. Spot trends, embrace original movements and be the first to try something new. You never know, it could be the making of your own career, your own future or just your own enjoyment.

Social media is not going away, so why not embrace it? Be social. Use your voice, join a community and use the tools that technology has offered you. Instagram, Twitter, YouTube and Pinterest – they're all breeding grounds for creativity, opinions and new ideas, so use them for their best parts, leave the worst parts and then learn, play and grow. If you want to develop a following, or if you just want to Be accessible and easy to find for your peers, your potential audience or the people who share your interests, ensure they can find you in all the noise. You might not want to be present on every channel, but choose your favourites and make use of the digital space. Start a blog, open an online store, go global or reach a new audience with a #ad.

Stay ahead of the game, learn the new rules and make the most of your opportunities. This world is there for the taking.

Index

Picture credits

All images of Victoria, other than the photographers listed below: @harrison

pp 6 (bottom right), 13 (left), 22, 27, 41, 43, 53, 87, 96, 120, 121, 128, 148, 151 (right), 202 (left), 251, 253 @ inthefrow; p 13 (right) @cgstreetstyle; p 20 © Clem Onojeghuo/Unsplash.com; p 23 David Paul Morris/Bloomberg via Getty Images; p 24 mubus7/Shutterstock.com; p 25 pio3/Shutterstock.com; p 29 Steve Azzara/Corbis via Getty Images; p 30 Andisheh Eslamboli/REX/Shutterstock; p 31 REUTERS/Suzanne Plunkett; p 34 Matthew Lloyd/Bloomberg via Getty Images; p 46 @rawpixel/Unsplash.com; p 50 Strathberry Collaboration Imagery; p 57 @benjaminrobyn/Unsplash.com; p 58 Billion Photos/Shutterstock.com; p 59 Sofie Delauw/Getty Images; p 64 Bauer-Griffin/GC Images/Getty Images; p 66 Victor Virgile/Gamma-Rapho via Getty Images; p 68 John Sciulli/Getty Images for Calvin Klein; p 73 Edward Simons/Alamy Stock Photo; p 74 Matt Cardy/Getty Images; p 84 © Zabulon Laurent/ABACA/PA Images; p 86 David Fisher/REX/Shutterstock; p 91 © Shutterstock.com; pp 95, 114, 115 @kylegalvin; p 101 Gabriel Bouys/AFP/Getty Images; p 102 @amberrosephoto; p 103 Zak Waters/Alamy Stock Photo; p 109 (left) Kirstin Sinclair/FilmMagic/Getty Images; p 109 (right) Jared Siskin/Patrick McMullan via Getty Images; p 116 @valentinfougeray; p 119 Kirstin Sinclair/Getty Images; p 127 Tullio Puglia/Getty Images; p 140 Pascal Le Segretain/Getty Images; p 143 Douglas Kirkland/Sygma/Corbis via Getty Images; p 145 (left) JP Yim/Getty Images; p 145 (right) Bertrand Rindoff Petroff/Getty Images; p 147 David M. Benett/Dave Benett/Getty Images for Stella McCartney; p 150 (left) @amelialiana; p 150 (right) @hallooctober; p 155 (left) @heatherribberson; p 155 (right) Wayne Tippetts/Alamy Stock Photo; p 156 @georgecraigono; p 157 @salihsworld; p 158 Jo Davidson/REX/Shutterstock; p 160 David M. Benett/Dave Benett/Getty Images; p 161 Swan Gallet/WWD/REX/Shutterstock; p 162 Victor Virgile/Gamma-Rapho via Getty Images; p 166 Raymond Hall/GC Images/Getty Images; p 168 © Ian Davidson/NEWZULU/Alamy Live News; p 172 David Crotty/Patrick McMullan via Getty Images; p 174 Frazer Harrison/Getty Images for Mercedes-Benz; p 178 REX/Shutterstock; p 179 Jared Siskin/Patrick McMullan via Getty Images; p 180 © Stas May; p 181 Sean Zanni/Patrick McMullan via Getty Images; p 182 Alberto Pezzali/NurPhoto via Getty Images; p 183 Vittorio Zunino Celotto/Getty Images; p 184 Estrop/Getty Images; p 189 Stephen Hilger/Bloomberg via Getty Images; p 190 @lefterisk/Unsplash.com; p 194 Casimiro Alamy Stock Photo; p 196 knape/Getty Images; p 198 Ann Johansson/Corbis via Getty Images; p 202 (right) Mike Marsland/WireImage/Getty Images; p 203 Christian Vierig/Getty Images; p 206 Vittorio Zunino Celotto/Getty Images; p 208 Jamie McCarthy/Getty Images; p 215-16 © Cameron-James Wilson; p 219 Michel Dufour/WireImage/Getty Images; p 222 @catmeffan; p 224 @katsfilm; p 229 Pixelformula/SIPA/REX/Shutterstock; p 230 (left) Anton Oparin/Alamy Stock Photo; (right) Timur Emek/Getty Images; p 232 Gareth Cattermole/Getty Images; p 234 Vittorio Zunino Celotto/Getty Images; p 235 Edward Berthelot/Getty Images; p 242 David M. Benett/Dave Benett/Getty Images; p 244 Damon Baker/Glamour © The Condé Nast Publications Ltd; p 254 Jonas Gustavsson/SIPA USA/PA Images; p 257 Stephane Cardinale/Corbis via Getty Images; p 258 Bertrand-Hillion Marie-Paola/ABACA/PA Images; p 260 (left) @ownwayofinspiration; p 260 (right) @mikkoputtonen; p 262 Joachim Ladefoged/Gallery Stock; p 271 @philltaylormade

While every effort has been made to trace the owners of copyright material reproduced herein and secure permissions, the publishers would like to apologise for any omissions and will be pleased to incorporate missing acknowledgements in any future edition of this book.

Acknowledgements

This book absolutely wouldn't have been possible without the following wonderful people. My loyal and supportive audience of fashion and beauty lovers. You guys lift me up when I need it but permanently keep my feet firmly on the ground. Thank you to HarperCollins especially, for believing in my vision and understanding my love of the online fashion world. My team at Gleam Futures, who are always there to keep me on the right track and have supported my ideas throughout our years together. Rebecca, for being my biggest source of inspiration and for never getting bored of being my platform to bounce ideas off. Steph, for knowing me better than I know myself. Kyle Galvin, for his knowledge, enthusiasm and imagination. Mum and Dad, for 29 years of endless love and support. And Alex, my love, for bringing me coffees in bed whenever I just needed time to write in my pyjamas.

About the author

Victoria Magrath is the creator and author of the award-winning fashion, travel and beauty blog, Inthefrow. Victoria established her blog in 2012 as she was completing her PhD at the University of Manchester on the impact of e-commerce on consumers' behaviour, following her role there as a Fashion Retailing lecturer. Within the six years of her blogging career, Victoria has won seven awards including the UK's Best Fashion Blog of 2017.

Victoria has been the face of Hugo Boss's A/W17 campaign and Ted Baker's Christmas 2017 campaign. In 2017 Victoria became a Beauty Ambassador for L'Oreal Paris, starring in the Princes Trust campaign to champion confidence in young people. In 2018 Victoria became a regular fashion columnist for *Glamour* magazine and launched her first collection collaboration with luxury leather goods brand Strathberry. This is her first book.

inthefrow.com

@inthefrow